RETURN OF THE NAMES OF THE OFFICERS
IN THE ARMY,

RETURN OF THE NAMES OF THE OFFICERS
IN THE ARMY,

Who receive PENSIONS for the loss of Limbs, or for Wounds; specifying, the Rank they held at the time they were wounded, their present Rank, the nature of the Cases, the Places where, and the year when wounded, the amount of their Pensions, and the Dates from which they commence.

War-Office,
30th April 1818.

PALMERSTON.

Ordered, by The House of Commons, *to be Printed,*
14 *May* 1818.

Published by

The Naval & Military Press Ltd
Unit 5 Riverside, Brambleside
Bellbrook Industrial Estate
Uckfield, East Sussex
TN22 1QQ England

Tel: +44 (0)1825 749494

www.naval-military-press.com
www.nmarchive.com

In reprinting in facsimile from the original, any imperfections are inevitably reproduced and the quality may fall short of modern type and cartographic standards.

NAMES OF THE OFFICERS IN THE ARMY, WHO RECEIVE

REGIMENTS.	NAMES.	Rank when Wounded.	Present Rank.
R¹ Horse Guards	Hill, Sir Robert	Lᵗ Colonel	Lᵗ Colonel
- - Do - -	Elley, Sir John	Lᵗ Colonel	Colonel
- - Do - -	Varley, Thomas	Quarter Master	Quarter Master
1st Dragoon Guards	Balcomb, J.	Captain	Sold out as Major in 1805
- - Do - -	Turner, Michael	Major	Major
- - Do - -	Harris, Thoˢ Noel	Captain	Brevet Major
- - Do - -	Sweny, John Paget	Captain	Captain
2d Dragoon Guards	Craufurd, Charles	Lᵗ Colonel	Lᵗ General
3d Dragoon Guards	Brice, George Tito	Captain	Major
6th Dragoon Guards	Stephens, Peter	Lieutenant	No longer in the Service
1st Dragoons	Radclyffe, Charles Edward	Captain	Brevet Lᵗ Colonel
- - Do - -	Gunning, George	Lieutenant	Lieutenant
2d Dragoons	Vernor, Robert	Major	Sold out
6th Dragoons	Miller, Fiennes S.	Major Commanding	Sold out
- - Do - -	Browne, William Frederick	Captain	Captain
7th Light Dragoons	Heyliger, Peter Augustus	Captain	Captain
- - Do - -	Beatty, Frederick	Lieutenant	Lieutenant
8th Light Dragoons	Willard, Leonard K.	Lieutenant	Captain
9th Light Dragoons	Gore, George	Captain	Lᵗ Colonel
10th Light Dragoons	Synge, Charles	Lieut. & Aide de Camp	Brevet Major
11th Light Dragoons	King, Charles	Lieutenant	Captain
12th Light Dragoons	Archdall, Mervyn	Lᵗ Colonel	Lᵗ General
- - - Do -	Ponsonby, Hon. Frederick C.	Colonel	Colonel
13th Light Dragoons	Smith, William Haytor	Lieutenant	Lieutenant
- - - Do -	Bowers, Charles Robert	Lieutenant	Lieutenant
14th Light Dragoons	Hervey, F. B.	Major	Colonel
15th Light Dragoons	Dalrymple, Leighton C.	Lᵗ Colonel	Lᵗ Colonel
- - - Do -	Thackwell, Joseph	Major	Brevet Lᵗ Colonel
16th Light Dragoons	Hay, James	Lᵗ Colonel	Lᵗ Colonel
17th Light Dragoons	Delancey, Oliver	Cornet	Lieutenant
18th Light Dragoons	Hesse, Charles	Lieutenant	Captain
19th Light Dragoons	Bailey, Philip	Lieutenant	Lieutenant
- - - Do -	- - Do -	- - Do -	- - Do -
- - - Do -	Wilson, Nathan	Captain	Major
22d Light Dragoons	Lumley, Hon. William	Lᵗ Colonel	Lᵗ General
23d Light Dragoons	Howard, Thomas Phipps	Captain	Major
- - - Do -	Wall, Thomas Barker	Lieutenant	Lieutenant
24th Light Dragoons	Webb, William	Lieutenant	Sold out
25th Light Dragoons	Ellis, Robert	Lᵗ Colonel	Brevet Lᵗ Colonel
1st Foot Guards	Ludlow, George Earl of	Captain and Lᵗ Colonel	General
- - Do - -	Wynyard, Edward	Assᵗ Adjutant General	Lᵗ Colonel
- - Do - -	Blunt, Francis Scawen	Ensign	No longer in the Service
- - Do - -	Bourke, Richard	Ensign	Colonel
- - Do - -	Woodforde, John	Lieutenant	Lᵗ Colonel
- - Do - -	Perceval, Philip Joshua	Lieuᵗ and Captain	Captain
- - Do - -	Lindsay, Hon. James	Lieuᵗ and Captain	Captain
- - Do - -	Cameron, William Gordon	Ensign	Lieutenant and Captain
- - Do - -	Cooke, Richard Harvey	Captain and Lᵗ Colonel	Captain and Lᵗ Colonel
- - Do - -	Cameron, William Gordon	Captain	Lieutenant and Captain
- - Do - -	Burges, Somerville W.	Captain	Sold out
- - Do - -	Somerset, Lord Fitzroy	Colonel	Brevet Colonel
- - Do - -	Stuart, Hon. William	Colonel	Brevet Colonel
2d Foot Guards	Bayly, H.	Ensign	Major General
- - Do - -	Fearon, Henry	Assistant Surgeon	Assistant Surgeon
- - Do - -	- - Do -	- - Do -	- - Do -
- - Do - -	Frazer, Charles	Lieutenant	No longer in the Service
- - Do - -	Walpole, Hon. J.	Lieutenant	Lᵗ Colonel
- - Do - -	Chaplin, Thomas	Ensign	Captain
- - Do - -	Anstruther, Wyndham	Ensign	Captain
- - Do - -	Gillham, John Allen	Surgeon	Surgeon
- - Do - -	Wyndham, Henry	Lᵗ Colonel	Lᵗ Colonel
3d Foot Guards	Ansley, Benjamin	Lieuᵗ and Captain	Lᵗ Colonel
- - Do - -	Cunyngham, David	Lieuᵗ and Captain	Colonel
- - Do - -	Knox, John	Ensign	No longer in the Service
- - Do - -	Geils, Thomas	Lieutenant	Lᵗ Colonel
- - Do - -	Evelyn, George	Lieuᵗ and Captain	Lieutenant and Captain
1st Foot	Logan, Abraham	Captain	Captain
- - Do -	Sneath, Thomas	Quarter Master	Lieutenant
- - Do -	Arguimbeau, Lawrence	Major Commanding	Brevet Lᵗ Colonel
- - Do -	Stoyte, John	Lieutenant	Lieutenant

PENSIONS FOR THE LOSS OF LIMBS, &c.

Nature of the Cases.	PLACES WHERE, And year when Wounded.	Amount.	Date of Commencement.
		£.	
for a wound	Waterloo - 1815	* 300	19th June - 1816.
for wounds	Waterloo - 1815	* 300	19th June - 1816.
for a wound	Waterloo - 1815	* 50	19th June - 1816.
for wounds	Anheim - 1794	100	25th December - 1811.
for a wound	Waterloo - 1815	* 200	19th June - 1816.
loss of an arm	Waterloo - 1815	200	19th June - 1816.
for wounds	Waterloo - 1815	* 100	19th June - 1816.
for wounds	Amberg - 1796	400	25th December - 1811.
for wounds	Talavera - 1809	100	25th December - 1811.
for a wound	Ireland - 1798	70	25th December - 1811.
for a wound	Waterloo - 1815	* 100	19th June - 1816.
for a wound	Waterloo - 1815	* 70	19th June - 1816.
for wounds	Waterloo - 1815	* 200	19th June - 1816.
for a wound	Waterloo - 1815	* 300	19th June - 1816.
for wounds	Waterloo - 1815	* 100	19th June - 1816.
for a wound	Waterloo - 1815	* 100	19th June - 1816.
for a wound	Waterloo - 1815	* 70	19th June - 1816.
loss of an arm	Lasswaree - 1803	100	25th December - 1811.
for wounds	Afzulghar - 1805	100	25th December - 1811.
for a wound	Salamanca - 1812	100	23d July - 1813.
loss of an arm	Fuente Guinaldo - 1811	100	26th September - 1812.
loss of an arm	Alexandria - 1801	400	25th December - 1811.
for wounds	Waterloo - 1815	" 300	19th June - 1816.
for wounds	Campo Mayor - 1811	* 70	25th March - 1812.
for a wound	Waterloo - 1815	* 70	19th June - 1816.
loss of an arm	Douro - 1809	300	25th December - 1811.
loss of a leg	Waterloo - 1815	300	19th June - 1816.
loss of an arm	Waterloo - 1815	300	19th June - 1816.
for a wound	Waterloo - 1815	* 300	19th June - 1816.
loss of an arm	East Indies - 1815	50	25th December - 1816.
for a wound	Waterloo - 1815	* 70	19th June - 1816.
loss of sight	East Indies - 1799	70	25th December - 1811.
- - D° -	- D° -	70	- - D°.
for a wound	Assaye - 1803	* 100	25th December - 1811.
loss of the use of a limb	Antrim - 1798	400	25th December - 1811.
for a wound	Talavera - 1809	200	25th December - 1811.
loss of a leg	Waterloo - 1815	70	19th June - 1816.
Injury sustained in the performance of military duty	Bhurtpore - 1805	* 70	25th December - 1811.
- - - D° - - D° -	Lasswaree - 1803	* 300	25th December - 1815.
loss of an arm	Flanders - 1794	400	25th December - 1811.
for wounds	St. Maura - 1810	300	25th December - 1811.
for wounds	Corunna - 1809	50	25th December - 1811.
for wounds	Holland - 1799	50	25th December - 1811.
for wounds	Corunna - 1809	* 100	25th December - 1811.
for wounds	Bayonne - 1814	* 100	19th May - 1815.
for a wound	Bergen-op-Zoom - 1814	* 100	10th March - 1815.
for wounds	Barrosa - 1811	* 100	6th March - 1812.
for a wound	Waterloo - 1815	* 300	19th June - 1816.
loss of an arm	Waterloo - 1815	100	19th June - 1816.
loss of a leg	Waterloo - 1815	100	19th June - 1816.
loss of an arm	Waterloo - 1815	300	19th June - 1816.
loss of an arm	Quatre Bras - 1815	300	17th June - 1816.
for wounds	Lincelles - 1793	50	25th December - 1811
loss of sight	Egypt - 1801	50	25th December - 1811.
- - D° -	- D° -	50	- - D°.
loss of a leg	Burgos - 1812	100	24th September - 1813.
for a wound	Burgos - 1812	100	19th October - 1813.
for wounds	St. Sebastian - 1813	50	1st September - 1814.
for wounds	St. Jean de Luz - 1813	* 50	11th November - 1814.
loss of sight	Egypt - 1801	100	25th December - 1811.
for a wound	Waterloo - 1815	* 300	19th June - 1816.
for wounds	Egypt - 1801	300	25th December - 1811.
for wounds	Lincelles - 1793	* 100	25th December - 1811.
for wounds	Burgos - 1812	70	18th October - 1813
for wounds	Talavera - 1809	* 100	25th December - 1811.
for a wound	Waterloo - 1815	* 100	19th June - 1816.
loss of an arm	St. Sebastian - 1813	100	24th July - 1814.
loss of an eye	Demerara - 1809	50	25th December - 1811.
loss of an arm	St. Sebastian - 1813	300	26th July - 1814.
for a wound	Bergen-op-Zoom - 1814	* 70	9th March - 1815.

(continued)

REGIMENTS.	NAMES.	Rank when Wounded.	Present Rank.
1st Foot	Rowan, James	Brevet Major	Brevet Major
- - D°	Bird, Edward Michael	Captain	Major
- - D°	Wilson, John	Captain	Brevet Lt Colonel
- - D°	Lorimer, Charles Hunt	Lieutenant	Lieutenant
- - D°	Macdonald, Coll.	Captain	Sold out as Major
- - D°	Macdonald, Robert	Captain	Brevet Major
- - D°	Cooper, Leonard Morse	Ensign	Lieutenant
- - D°	Clarke, William	Lieutenant	Lieutenant
- - D°	Lane, George	Lieutenant	Lieutenant
- - D°	Mudie, Charles	Lieutenant	Lieutenant
- - D°	Alston, James	Ensign	Lieutenant
2d Foot	Hutton, William	Lieutenant	Lieutenant
3d Foot	Woods, Richard	Lieutenant	Captain
- - D°	Latham, Matthew	Lieutenant	Captain
- - D°	D° - - D°	- - D°	- D° -
- - D°	Blake, Robert	Lieutenant	Lieutenant
- - D°	Hooper, Richard	Lieutenant	Captain
- - D°	West, John Taaffe	Lieutenant	Lieutenant
- - D°	Cameron, Charles	Captain	Major
4th Foot	Barron, Edward	Lieutenant	Captain
- - D°	Edgell, Charles James	Captain	Captain
- - D°	Gichard, Edward	Lieutenant	Lieutenant
- - D°	Piper, John	Lt Colonel	Brevet Lt Colonel
- - D°	Burke, Thomas	Captain	Major
- - D°	Browne, John	Lieutenant	Captain
- - D°	Alley, William Henry	Lieutenant	Captain
- - D°	Buchannan, James Armstrong	Lieutenant	Lieutenant
- - D°	D° - - D°	- - D°	- - D°
- - D°	Williamson, John	Major	Major
- - D°	Faunce, A. D.	Major	Brevet Lt Colonel
- - D°	Benwell, Thomas	Ensign	Lieutenant
- - D°	Andrews, Henry	Lieutenant	Lieutenant
- - D°	Brooke, Henry William	Lieutenant	Lieutenant
- - D°	Richardson, George	Lieutenant	Lieutenant
- - D°	Browne, John	Lieutenant	Captain
5th D°	Hamilton, Nicholas	Captain	Major
- - D°	Williams, William	Ensign	Lieutenant
- - D°	D° - - D°	D°	
- - D°	Ayshford, Aaron Moore	Ensign	Lieutenant
- - D°	Bennett, Alexander Maxwell	Captain	Brevet Major
- - D°	Clerke, Thomas Henry Shadwell	Lieutenant	Captain
- - D°	Hopkins, W. R.	Ensign	Lieutenant
- - D°	Dubourdieu, Arthur	Captain	Captain
- - D°	Doyle, Michael Taylor	Captain	Captain
- - D°	Pennington, Rowland	Lieutenant	Lieutenant
- - D°	Boulger, Persse O'Keefe	Ensign	Major
- - D°	- - D° - -	Major	- D° -
- - D°	Wylde, John Newman	Lieutenant	Captain
6th Ditto	Blood, Thomas	Ensign	Lieutenant
- - D°	Smith, Samuel De la Chervis	Captain	Captain
7th Ditto	Magennis, Richard	Captain	Captain
- - D°	Mair, John	Captain	Captain
- - D°	Healy, John	Lieutenant	Lieutenant
- - D°	Gibbons, F.	Lieutenant	Captain
- - D°	Mullins, Thomas J. Arenburg	Lieutenant	Captain
- - D°	Devey, Henry Fryer	Lieutenant	Captain
- - D°	Holden, John Fish	Lieutenant	No longer in the Service
- - D°	Orr, John	Captain	Major
- - D°	Loggan, George	Lieutenant	Captain
8th Ditto	Fortye, Thomas	Captain	Major
- - D°	Duke, Alexander	Major	No longer in the Service
- - D°	Mundy, James	Captain	No longer in the Service
- - D°	Blackmore, John	Major	Major
- - D°	Mundy, James	Major	No longer in the Service

PENSIONS FOR THE LOSS OF LIMBS, &c.

Nature of the Cases.	PLACES WHERE, And year when Wounded.	Amount. £.	Date of Commencement.
for wounds	Fort Erie - 1814	200	16th August - 1815.
for wounds	Chippawa - 1814	* 100	6th July - 1815.
for wounds	Chippawa - 1814	* 100	6th July - 1815.
for wounds	Corunna - 1809	* 70	25th December - 1811.
for a wound	Calvi - 1794	* 100	25th December - 1811.
for a wound	Waterloo - 1815	250	19th June - 1816.
for wounds	Quatre Bras - 1815	* 50	17th June - 1816.
for a wounds	Quatre Bras - 1815	* 70	17th June - 1816.
loss of an arm	Waterloo - 1815	70	19th June - 1816.
ruptured	Waterloo - 1815	50	19th June - 1816.
for wounds	St. Sebastian - 1813	* 50	26th July - 1814.
for wounds	Pampeluna - 1813	* 70	29th July - 1814.
loss of a leg	Albuera - 1811	100	17th May - 1812.
loss of an arm	Albuera - 1811	100	17th May - 1812.
for wounds	- Dº -	70	Dº.
loss of a leg	Bayonne - 1813	100	14th December - 1814.
for wounds	Albuera - 1811	*70	17th May - 1812.
Injury sustained in the performance of military duty	France - 1816	70	31st October - 1817.
for wounds	Egmont-op-Zee - 1799 Albuera - 1811 Nivelle - 1813 Bayonne - 1813 France - 1814	100	25th December - 1816.
for wounds	Bunker's Hill - 1775	70	25th December - 1811.
for wounds	Vittoria - 1813	* 100	22d June - 1814.
for wounds	Bayonne - 1813	* 70	11th December - 1814.
for wounds	Bayonne - 1813	300	12th December - 1814.
for wounds	Badajos - 1812	* 100	7th April - 1813.
for wounds	Badajos - 1812	70	7th April - 1813.
for wounds	Badajos - 1812	* 70	7th April - 1813.
for wounds	Bladensburgh - 1814	70	25th August - 1815.
- - Dº -	- - Dº - -	* 70	- - Dº.
for wounds	Badajos - 1812	200	7th April - 1813.
for wounds	New Orleans - 1815	* 200	9th January - 1816.
for wounds	New Orleans - 1815	* 50	9th January - 1816.
for wounds	New Orleans - 1815	* 70	9th January - 1816.
for a wound	New Orleans - 1815	* 70	9th January - 1816.
for a wound	Waterloo - 1815	70	19th June - 1816.
for a wound	Waterloo - 1815	100 {2ᵈ Pension}	19th June - 1816.
loss of a leg	Flushing - 1809	200	25th December - 1811.
for wounds more than equal to loss of limb	Sabugal - 1811	70	4th April - 1812.
	- Dº -	70	- - Dº.
for wounds	Ciudad Rodrigo - 1812	* 70	17th January - 1813.
for wounds	Badajos - 1812	* 100	7th April - 1813.
loss of a leg	Redinha - 1811	100	13th March - 1812.
for wounds	Badajos - 1812	* 50	7th April - 1813.
for wounds	Ciudad Rodrigo - 1812	* 100	20th January - 1813.
for wounds	Badajos - 1812	* 100	7th April - 1813.
for wounds	Orthes - 1814	* 70	25th February - 1815.
for wounds	Holland - 1799	50	25th December - 1811.
for wounds	New Orleans - 1815	*200	9th January - 1816.
for a wound	Ciudad Rodrigo - 1812	* 70	20th January - 1813.
for wounds	Orthes - 1814	* 50	28th February - 1815.
for a wound	Fort Erie - 1814	* 100	17th September - 1815.
loss of an arm	Albuera - 1811	100	16th May - 1812.
for wounds	Badajos - 1812	100	7th April - 1813.
loss of an arm	Albuera - 1811	70	17th May - 1812.
for a wound	Albuera - 1811	* 70	17th May - 1812.
for a wound	Albuera - 1811	100	17th May - 1812.
for wounds	Badajos - 1812	100	7th April - 1813.
for wounds	Albuera - 1811	* 70	17th May - 1812.
for wounds	Albuera - 1811	* 200	17th May - 1812.
for wounds	Pampeluna - 1813	* 100	29th July - 1814.
loss of an arm	Egypt - 1801	200	25th December - 1811.
for wounds	Egypt - 1801	* 200	25th December - 1811.
for wounds	America - 1813	200	6th June - 1814.
for wounds	America - 1813	100	30th May - 1814.
for wounds	America - 1813	200 {2ᵈ Pension}	6th June - 1814.

(continued.)

NAMES OF THE OFFICERS IN THE ARMY, WHO RECEIVE

REGIMENTS.	NAMES.	Rank when Wounded.	Present Rank.
9th Foot	Lindsay, George	Lieutenant	Lieutenant
- - D°	Godwin, Henry	Captain	Major
- - D°	Shelton, John	Captain	Captain
- - D°	Ackland, John	Lieutenant	Captain
- - D°	Sheppard, Thomas	Lieutenant	Lieutenant
- - D°	- - - D° - -	- - D° -	- - D° -
- - D°	Sankey, Samuel	Captain	Major
- - D°	Holmes, David	Ensign	Lieutenant
- - D°	Ruse, Richard	Lieutenant	Lieutenant
- - D°	Campbell, Colin	Captain	Captain
- - D°	Dumaresq, Henry	Captain	Captain
- - D°	Gomm, Sir William	Major	Captain and Lt Col. 2d Foot Guards
10th Ditto	Rolston, Thomas	Ass^t Surgeon	Assistant Surgeon
11th Ditto	Mac Gregor, William Gordon	Major	Lt Colonel
- - D°	Cuyler, George	Lt Colonel	Colonel
- - D°	Williams, James	Lieutenant	Captain
- - D°	Smith, Jenkin Boys	Lieutenant	Lieutenant
- - D°	Trimble, Matthew	Ensign	Ensign
- - D°	Porter, James	Captain	Captain
12th Ditto	Nixon, Robert	Captain	Brevet Lt Colonel
- - D°	Ashe, William Hoadly	Lieutenant	Captain
14th Ditto	Hope, Honourable Alexander	Lt Colonel	Lt General
15th Ditto	Machell, Christopher	Lt Colonel	Sold out
16th Ditto	Bowen, Henry	Ensign	Major
- - D°	Hargrove, John L.	Lieutenant	Lieutenant
17th D°	Wynn, Sir William	Lieutenant	Captain
- - D°	Grace, Michael John	Captain	Captain
- - D°	- - - D° - -	- D° - -	- D° - -
- - D°	Poyntz, Arthur	Lieutenant	Captain
20th Ditto	Hamilton, Christopher	Lieutenant	Lt Colonel
- - D°	Bainbrigge, J H.	Lieutenant	Captain
- - D°	De Voeux, Charles	Lieutenant	Captain, on Half-pay, 63d Foot
- - D°	Telford, Robert	Captain	Captain
- - D°	Murray, John	Captain	Major
- - D°	Smith, David Augustus	Captain	Captain
- - D°	Maister, John	Captain	Colonel
- - D°	Hoath, Charles	Quarter Master	Quarter Master
21st Foot	Mackenzie, Donald	Captain	Captain
- - D°	Adam, Sir Frederick	Colonel	M. General
- - D°	Ross, Alexander James	Major	Major
- - D°	Paterson, William	Lt Colonel	Lt Colonel
- - D°	French, Anthony	Captain	Sold out as B^t. Lt Col.
- - D°	Henry, Robert	Major	- - - D°
- - D°	Quin, Peter	Lieutenant	Lieutenant
22d D°	Creswell, William	Lieutenant	Captain
- - D°	D° - - D°	- - D° -	- - D° -
- - D°	Lindsay, Effingham	Captain	B^t Lt Colonel
23d D°	Treeve, Richard	Lieutenant	Captain
- - D°	Tucker, Thomas Edwardes	Lieutenant	Captain
- - D°	Harrison, John Christopher	Lieutenant	Captain
- - D°	Herford, William Lewis	Captain	B^t Lt Colonel
- - D°	Cochrane, Thomas	Lieutenant	Captain
- - D°	Leahy, John Thomas	Captain	Major
- - D°	Booker Gordon, William Francis	Lieutenant	Captain
- - D°	Browne, George	Lieutenant	Captain
- - D°	Holmes, Robert Pattison	Lieutenant	Lieutenant
- - D°	Cochrane, Thomas	Lieutenant	Captain
- - D°	Hill, J. H. E.	Major	B^t Lt Colonel
24th D°	Skene, Alexander	Lieutenant	Captain
- - D°	Baird, Sir David	Lt General	General
- - D°	Stack, George	Lieutenant	Captain
- - D°	Tudor, William	Lieutenant	Captain
25th D°	Hockings, Richard	Lieutenant	Lieutenant
- - D°	Brown, Samuel	Lieutenant	Lieutenant
- - D°	Light, Alexander Whalley	Lieutenant	Lt Colonel

Nature of the Cases.	PLACES WHERE, And year when Wounded.		Amount.	Date of Commencement.	
			£.		
loss of an arm	Busaco	1810	70	25th December	1811.
loss of the use of a hand	Barrosa	1811	200	6th March	1812.
loss of an arm	St. Sebastian	1813	100	1st July	1814.
loss of the use of a hand	Burgos	1812	100	26th October	1813.
for a wound	Adour	1813	70	8th October	1814.
- - Dº	- Dº -	-	70	- - Dº. - -	
for wounds	Roleia	1808	* 100	25th December	1811.
for wounds	Pyrennees	1813	* 50	12th December	1814.
loss of an eye	St. Sebastian	1813	70	18th July	1814.
for wounds	St. Sebastian	1813	* 100	26th July	1814.
for wounds	Waterloo	1815	* 100	19th June	1816.
for a wound	Bidart	1813	300	10th December	1814.
loss of a leg	Tarragona	1813	70	8th August	1814.
for wounds	Salamanca	1812	200	23 July	1813.
for wounds	Salamanca	1812	* 300	23 July	1813.
for wounds	Salamanca	1812	* 100	23 July	1813.
for wounds	Salamanca	1812	* 70	23 July	1813.
for wounds	Nivelle	1813	50	11th November	1814.
for a wound	Salamanca	1812	* 100	23d July	1813.
for wounds	Seringapatam	1799	100	25th December	1811.
for wounds	Bourbon	1810	100	25th December	1811.
loss of the use of an arm	Holland	1795	400	25th December	1811.
loss of an arm	N. America	1776	100	25th December	1811.
loss of a leg	America	1780	200	25th December	1811.
loss of hearing	Martinique	-	50	25th December	1814.
for wounds	Holland	1799	100	25th December	1811.
loss of a leg	Holland	1799	100	25th December	1811.
for other wounds	- Dº -	-	50	- - Dº.	
for wounds	Nepaul	1815	* 70	3d January	1816.
loss of a leg	Holland	1799	300	25th December	1811.
loss of an arm	Pampeluna	1813	100	29th July	1814.
loss of a leg	Holland	1799	100	25th December	1811.
for wounds	Orthes	1814	* 100	28th February	1815.
for wounds	Orthes	1814	200	28th February	1815.
for wounds	Orthes	1814	* 100	28th February	1815.
for wounds	Holland	1799	* 100	25th December	1811.
loss of an eye	-	1813	50	25th December	1814.
loss of a leg	Bergen-op-Zoom	1814	100	9th March	1815.
for wounds	Ordall	1813	* 300	14th September	1814.
for wounds	New Orleans	1815	* 200	9th January	1816.
for wounds	New Orleans	1815	* 300	9th January	1816.
loss of an eye	Sicily	1807	300	25th December	1811.
for a wound	Bergen-op-Zoom	1814	* 200	9th March	1815.
loss of an eye	New Orleans	1815	70	9th January	1816.
loss of an eye	Bhurtpore	1805	100	25th December	1811.
for other wounds	- - Dº	-	70	- - Dº.	
loss of a leg	Bhurtpore	1805	300	25th December	1811.
for wounds	Albuera	1811	100	17th May	1812.
for wounds	Badajoz	1812	* 100	7th April	1813.
for wounds	Badajoz	1812	100	7th April	1813.
for wounds	Albuera	1811	* 300	17th May	1812.
for wounds	Bunkers Hill	1775	100	25th December	1811.
for wounds	Badajoz	1812	* 100	7th April	1813.
for wounds	Albuera	1811	70	17th May	1812.
for wounds	Roncevalles	1813	* 70	26th July	1814.
for wounds	Badajoz	1812	70	7th April	1813.
for wounds	{ Zelenhausen 1761 Bunker's Hill 1775 }		50, 2ᵈ Pension	25th December	1815.
for a wound	Waterloo	1815	* 200	19th June	1816.
loss of a leg	Talavera	1809	100	25th December	1811.
loss of an arm	Corunna	1809	450	25th December	1811.
loss of an arm	Orthes	1814	100	28th February	1812.
loss of an eye	-	1806	100	25th December	1811.
loss of a leg	Egypt	1801	100	25th December	1811.
for wounds	Merocem	1814	* 70	24th June	1815.
for wounds	Egmont-op-Zee	1809	* 300	25th December	1811.

(continued.)

NAMES OF THE OFFICERS IN THE ARMY, WHO RECEIVE

REGIMENTS.	NAMES.	Rank when Wounded.	Present Rank.
26th Foot	Maxwell, Sir William	Lt Colonel	No longer in the Service
— Do	Campbell, Charles Stuart	Captain	Major
27th Do	Graham, Samuel	Lt Colonel	Lt General
— Do	Do — Do	— Do	— Do
— Do	Pring, John	Captain	Captain
— Do	McMurdo, Archibald	Captain	No longer in the Service
— Do	Phillips, Robert J.	Ensign	Lieutenant
— Do	Drewe, John Ringrove	Lieutenant	Captain
— Do	Maclean, Sir John	Colonel	Colonel
— Do	Butler, William	Captain	Captain
— Do	Winser, William	Captain	Captain
— Do	Manley, Charles	Lieutenant	Lieutenant
— Do	Pollock, Carlisle	Lieutenant	Captain
— Do	Reeves, George James	Lt Colonel	Lt Colonel
— Do	Hill, Joseph	Lieutenant	Lieutenant
— Do	Geddes, John	Captain	Captain
— Do	Henderson, William	Lieutenant	Captain
— Do	M'Donnald, George	Lieutenant	Captain in 16th Foot
— Do	Millar, John	Lieutenant	Lieutenant
— Do	Fortescue, William Faithful	Lieutenant	Lieutenant
— Do	Phibbs, William Harlow	Lieutenant	Lieutenant
28th Do	Johnson, Edward	Assistant Surgeon	Surgeon
— Do	Wilkinson, John Frederick	Lieutenant	Lieutenant
— Do	Cottingham, Edward	Lieutenant	Captain
— Do	Bean, Isaac	Captain	Captain
— Do	Taylor, William Vere	Captain	Captain
— Do	Clark, John	Lieutenant	Lieutenant
— Do	Irving, William	Captain	Bt Lt Colonel
— Do	Llewellyn, Richard	Captain	Captain
— Do	Bowles, John	Captain	Captain
— Do	Wilson, Thomas	Captain	Captain
29th Do	Monsell Wilson	Lieutenant	Lieutenant
— Do	— Do	— Do	— Do
— Do	Arbuthnot, Sir Thomas	Ensign	Colonel
— Do	Kearney, Edward	Ensign	Lieutenant
— Do	Way, Sir Gregory, H. B.	Major	Lt Colonel
— Do	Tod, George	Captain	Major
— Do	Creagh Andrew	Captain	Lt Colonel
— Do	Stannus, Robert	Lieutenant	Captain
— Do	Hodge, Peter	Brevet Major	Lt Colonel
30th Do	Livingstone, Hay	Lieutenant	Captain
— Do	Turner, Charles	Lt Colonel	Colonel
— Do	Stewart, William	Captain	Major
— Do	Lockwood Purefoy	Lieutenant	Lieutenant
31st Do	King, Peter	Ensign	Ensign
— Do	Meade, Hon. Robert	Brigadier General	Lt General
— Do	Colman, George	Captain	Captain
— Do	Bray, Edmund Moore	Lieutenant	Captain
— Do	Nun, Loftus	Lieutenant	Lieutenant
— Do	Raymond, William	Lieutenant	Lieutenant
— Do	M'Intosh, Andrew	Quarter Master	Lieutenant
— Do	Girdlestone, John	Captain	Captain
— Do	Anderson, Paul	Captain	Colonel
— Do	Blomer, Charles	Captain	Captain
— Do	Gibson, William	Lieutenant	Lieutenant
— Do	Colman, George	Captain	Captain
— Do	Knox, Edward	Captain	Bt Major
— Do	Beamish, George	Lieutenant	Lieutenant
32d Do	Quill, Henry	Ensign	Lieutenant
— Do	Graves, Anthony	Lieutenant	Captain
— Do	Toole, William Henry	Captain	Major
— Do	Sweetman, Walter	Lieutenant	Captain Half-pay 90th Foot
— Do	Quill, Henry	Lieutenant	Lieutenant
— Do	Barr, George	Captain	Captain
— Do	Jagoe, Jonathan	Lieutenant	Lieutenant

PENSIONS FOR THE LOSS OF LIMBS, &c.

Nature of the Cases.	PLACES WHERE, And year when Wounded.	Amount. £.	Date of Commencement.
loss of an arm	Corunna - 1809	300	25th December - 1811.
for wounds	St. Sebastian - 1813	* 250	1st September - 1814.
loss of an eye	Holland - 1799	400	25th December - 1811.
for other wounds	- Dº -	400	- - Dº.
for wounds	Badajoz - 1811	* 100	11th May - 1812.
for wounds	Dominica - 1798	200	25th December - 1811.
for wounds	Badajoz - 1812	70	7th April - 1813.
loss of an arm	Pampeluna - 1813	100	29th July - 1814.
for wounds	Holland and Fort St. Christoval	300	11th April - 1815.
for wounds	Lezaca - 1813	100	2d August - 1814.
for wounds	Ordal - 1813	* 100	14th September - 1814.
for wounds	Ordal - 1813	* 70	14th September - 1814.
for wounds	Pampeluna - 1813	100	29th July - 1814.
for wounds	Ordal - 1813	300	14th September - 1814.
loss of an arm	Vittoria - 1813	70	22d June - 1814.
for wounds	Toulouse - 1814	* 100	11th April - 1815.
for a wound	Waterloo - 1815	* 100	19th June - 1816.
for wounds	Waterloo - 1815	* 70	19th June - 1816.
loss of an eye	Waterloo - 1815	70	19th June - 1816.
for a wound	Waterloo - 1815	70	19th June - 1816.
loss of an arm	Sarat - 1813	70	12th November - 1814.
for wounds	Spain - 1811	100	29th January - 1812.
for wounds	Barrosa - 1811	* 70	5th March - 1812.
loss of the use of an arm	Albuera - 1811	* 100	10th May - 1812.
Injury sustained in the performance of military duty	Ireland - 1809	100	25th December - 1811.
for wounds	Nive - 1813	100	10th December - 1814.
for wounds	Vittoria - 1813	* 70	22d June - 1814.
for a wound	Quatre Bras - 1815	* 300	17th June - 1816.
for wounds	Waterloo - 1815	* 300	19th June - 1816.
for a wound	Waterloo - 1815	100	19th June - 1816.
for a wound	Vittoria - 1813	* 100	22d June - 1814.
loss of sight	Canada - 1787	70	25th December - 1811.
- - Dº -	- Dº -	70	- - Dº.
for wounds	Grenada - 1796	300	25th December - 1811.
for wounds	Albuera - 1811	50	17th May - 1812.
for wounds	Albuera - 1811	* 200	17th May - 1812.
for wounds	Albuera - 1811	100	17th May - 1812.
for wounds	Vimiera - 1808	* 200	25th December - 1811.
for wounds	Talavera - 1809 and Albuera - 1811	* 70	17th May - 1812.
for wounds	Roleia - 1808	* 100	25th December - 1813.
loss of an eye	Corsica - 1794	100	25th December - 1811.
loss of an arm	Badajoz - 1811	300	10th May - 1812.
for wounds	Pampeluna - 1813	* 100	26th July - 1814.
for a wound	Quatre Bras - 1815	70	17th June - 1816.
loss of a leg	Holland - 1799	50	25th December - 1811.
loss of an eye	Rosetta - 1807	400	25th December - 1811.
for wounds	Talavera - 1809	100	25th December - 1811.
loss of sight	Egypt - 1807	* 100	25th December - 1811.
Injury sustained in the performance of military duty	Salamanca - 1812	70	13th November - 1813.
for wounds	Pyrenees - 1813	* 70	25th August - 1814.
for wounds	Pampeluna - 1813	50	29th July - 1814.
for wounds	St. Jean de Luz - 1813	100	11th November - 1814.
for wounds	Egypt - 1801	* 300	25th December - 1811.
Injury sustained in the performance of military duty	Egypt - 1807	100	25th December - 1811.
Injury sustained in the performance of military duty	Spain - 1814	* 70	10th January - 1815.
for a wound	Talavera - 1809	100 {2d Pension}	25th December - 1815.
loss of an arm	St. Palais - 1814	200	16th February - 1815.
Injury sustained on service	- - 1816	* 70	20th August - 1817.
loss of an eye	Burgos - 1812	70	12th October - 1813.
for wounds	Salamanca - 1812	100	23d July - 1813.
for wounds	Pampeluna - 1813	* 100	31st July - 1814.
Injury sustained in the performance of military duty	Spain - 1809	70	25th December - 1811.
for a wound	Quatre Bras - 1815	* 70	17th June - 1816.
for wounds	Waterloo - 1815	* 100	19th June - 1816.
for a wound	Waterloo - 1815	* 70	19th June - 1816.

(continued.)

REGIMENTS.	NAMES.	Rank when Wounded.	Present Rank.
33d Foot	Bannatyne, Frederick	Ensign	Lieutenant
- - D°	Pode, William	Lieutenant	Lieutenant
- - D°	Guthrie, John	Captain	No longer in the Service
- - D°	- - D°	- - D°	- - D°
- - D°	Kerr, Robert	Lieutenant	Capⁿ Half-pay 14th Foot
- - D°	Alderson, John	Lieutenant	Lieutenant
- - D°	Bain, William	Lieutenant	Lieutenant
- - D°	Forlong, James	Lieutenant	Lieutenant
- - D°	Canning, Edward	Lieutenant	Lieutenant
- - D°	Westmore, Richard	Lieutenant	Lieutenant
- - D°	Pagan, Samuel Alexander	Lieutenant	Lieutenant
34th D°	Fenwick, William	Lt Colonel	No longer in the Service
- - D°	Richardson, William	Lieutenant	Lieutenant
- - D°	Leeson, Honourable Robert	Lieutenant	Sold out as Captain
35th D°	Hay, Adam	Major	No longer in the Service
- - D°	Austin, Thomas	Lieutenant	Lieutenant
36th D°	M°Pherson, Evan	Ensign	Ensign
- - D°	Blakeney, Robert	Captain	Captain
- - D°	Tunstall, William	Lieutenant	Lieutenant
- - D°	Swain, William Wright	Captain	Major
- - D°	M°Cabe, James	Ensign	Ensign
- - D°	Prendergast, James	Lieutenant	Lieutenant
- - D°	Mackenzie, Alexander	Lt Colonel	Lt General
37th D°	Stowards, Robert	Lieutenant	Lieutenant
- - D°	Chapman, George	Ensign	Lieutenant
38th D°	Fullarton, Archibald	Captain	Captain
- - D°	Sandwich, Frederick Browne	Lieutenant	Captain
- - D°	Miles, Edward	Major Com^g	Lt Colonel
- - D°	Freer, George	Lieutenant	Lieutenant
- - D°	Walsh, Theodore	Ensign	Lieutenant
- - D°	Taylor, William	Captain	Major
- - D°	Campbell, Alexander	Lieutenant	Lieutenant
- - D°	Swiny, Shapland	Lieutenant	Lieutenant
- - D°	Peddie, John	Lieutenant	Captain
- - D°	Hewitt, J. H.	Lieutenant	B^t Lt Colonel
- - D°	Fraser, Alexander	Quarter Master	Lieutenant
39th D°	Lapslie, William Hart	Captain	Major
- - D°	Courtenay, William Allan	Ensign	Lieutenant
- - D°	Poe, Purefoy	Lieutenant	Lieutenant
- - D°	Brine, James	Captain	Captain
- - D°	Hart, Francis H.	Lieutenant	Lieutenant
- - D°	Rhodes, Robert	Ensign	Lieutenant
40th D°	Wickham, Joseph	Ensign	No longer in the Service
- - D°	Whetham, John	Captain	Major
- - D°	Southwell, Charles	Lieutenant	Captain
- - D°	Thompson, Joseph	Captain	No longer in the Service
- - D°	Gillies, John	Major	Lt Colonel
- - D°	Smith, Charles Hervey	Lieutenant	Captain
- - D°	Smith, Michael	Ensign	Lieutenant
- - D°	De Courcy, Honourable James	Lieutenant	Lieutenant
- - D°	Anthony, James	Lieutenant	Lieutenant
- - D°	Booth, George	Ensign	Ensign
- - D°	Glynn, James	Lieutenant	Lieutenant
- - D°	Harcourt, Charles Amedee	Lt Colonel	Colonel
- - D°	Brown, Honourable Michael	Lieutenant	Lieutenant
- - D°	Clarke, William Aldworth	Ensign	Ensign
- - D°	Thornhill, Richard	Ensign	Ensign
41st D°	Clemon, John	Lieutenant	Captain
- - D°	Saunders, Henry Caulfield	Captain	Captain
- - D°	Chambers, Peter Latouche	Captain	B^t Major
- - D°	Muir, Adam Charles	Captain	B^t Major
42d D°	Fraser, James Jonathan	Lieutenant	Major
- - D°	Stewart, William	Lieutenant	Captain

Nature of the Cases.	PLACES WHERE, And Year when Wounded.	Amount. £.	Date of Commencement.
loss of a leg	Bergen-op Zoom - 1814	70	9th March - 1815.
for wounds	Bergen-op-Zoom - 1814	* 70	10th March - 1815.
loss of an eye	Bergen-op-Zoom - 1814	200	9th March - 1815.
for other wounds	- - Do -	200	9th March - 1815.
for wounds	Bergen-op-Zoom - 1814	* 70	9th March - 1815.
loss of an arm	Quatre Bras - 1815	70	17th June - 1816.
for a wound	Waterloo - 1815	* 70	19th June - 1816.
for a wound	Quatre Bras - 1815	* 70	17th June - 1816.
for a wound	Bergen-op-Zoom - 1814	* 70	10th March - 1815.
for a wound	Waterloo - 1815	* 70	19th June - 1816.
for a wound	Waterloo - 1815	70	18th June - 1816.
loss of a leg	Pyrenees - 1813	300	26th July - 1814.
for wounds	Freemanstown - 1777	70	25th December - 1811.
for a wound	St. Vincent - 1796	70	25th December - 1811.
for wounds	Holland - 1799	200	25th December - 1811.
loss of a leg	Merxem - 1814	70	3d February - 1815.
loss of an eye	Foraish - 1813	50	25th March - 1814.
for a wound	Bayonne - 1813	* 100	11th November - 1814.
loss of an eye	St. Pé - 1813	70	11th November - 1814.
for a wound	Buenos Ayres - 1807	* 100	25th December - 1811.
for a wound	Toulouse - 1814	50	11th April - 1815.
for a wound	Toulouse - 1814	* 70	11th April - 1815.
loss of an eye	India - 1799	300	25th December - 1811.
loss of a leg	Merxem - 1814	100	5th February - 1815.
loss of a leg	Merxem - 1814	70	5th February - 1815.
loss of a leg	Salamanca - 1812	100	23d July - 1813.
loss of an arm	St. Sebastian - 1813	100	1st September - 1814.
for wounds	Salamanca - 1812	* 250	23d July - 1813.
for wounds	St. Sebastian - 1813 and Bayonne - 1813	* 70	10th December - 1814.
for wounds	St. Sebastian - 1813	* 50	26th July - 1814.
for wounds	Bayonne - 1813	* 100	10th December - 1814.
for wounds	Bayonne - 1814	100	17th March - 1815.
for wounds	America - 1775 / Do - 1778	70	25th December - 1811.
loss of an arm	Salamanca - 1812	100	23d July - 1813.
for a wound	Monte Video - 1807	70	25th December - 1811.
loss of an eye	Ireland - 1804	50	25th December - 1811.
for wounds	Calabria - 1808	200	25th December - 1811.
for wounds	Pyrenees - 1813	* 50	26th July - 1814.
for wounds	Pyrenees - 1813	* 70	26th July - 1814.
for wounds	Albuera - 1811	100	17th May - 1812.
for wounds	Albuera - 1811 / Pyrenees - 1813	* 70	17th May - 1812.
for a wound	Pyrenees - 1813	* 50	26th July - 1814.
loss of a leg	Egypt - 1801	50	25th December - 1811.
loss of a leg	Monte Video - 1807	200	25th December - 1811.
loss of a leg	Alexandria - 1801	100	25th December - 1811.
for wounds	Holland - 1799	200	25th December - 1811.
for wounds	Badajoz - 1812	300	7th April - 1813.
for wounds	Mont Video - 1807	70	25th December - 1811.
for wounds	Pampeluna - 1813	50	29th July - 1814.
loss of an arm	Brandywine - 1777	70	25th December - 1811.
for wounds	Badajoz - 1812 / Toulouse - 1814 / Waterloo - 1815	70	11th April - 1815.
for wounds	Pyrenees - 1813	50	11th November - 1814.
for wounds	Toulouse - 1814	* 70	11th April - 1815.
for a wound	Badajoz - 1812	300	7th April - 1813.
for a wound	Waterloo - 1815	70	19th June - 1816.
loss of an arm	Waterloo - 1815	50	19th June - 1816.
for a wound	Waterloo - 1815	* 50	19th June - 1816.
for wounds	Canada - 1813	* 70	23d January - 1814.
for wounds	America - 1813	* 200	12th July - 1814.
sight impaired	America - 1813	* 200	25th December - 1814.
injury sustained in the performance of military duty	Dublin - 1816	* 100	4th September - 1817.
for wounds	St. Lucia - 1796	200	25th December - 1811.
loss of the use of a leg	America - 1777	100	25th December - 1811.

(*continued.*)

REGIMENTS.	NAMES.	Rank when Wounded.	Present Rank.
42 Foot	Fraser, John	Captain	No longer in the Service
- - Dº	Menzies, Archibald	Captain	Major
- - Dº	Macpherson, Mungo	Captain	Captain
- - Dº	McDougall, Kennett	Lieutenant	Lieutenant
- - Dº	Fraser, Simon	Captain	Major
- - Dº	Stewart, James	Lt Colonel	No longer in the Service
- - Dº	Strange, Alexander	Lieutenant	Lieutenant
- - Dº	McKinnon, Ronald	Lieutenant	Lieutenant
- - Dº	McLaren, Charles	Lieutenant	Lieutenant
- - Dº	Stewart, Alexander	Lieutenant	Lieutenant
- - Dº	Stewart, John	Assistant Surgeon	Assistant Surgeon
- - Dº	Menzies, Archibald	Major	Major
- - Dº	McNiven, Thomas	Lieutenant	Lieutenant in 26th Foot
43d Dº	Frederick, Roger	Lieutenant	Captain
- - Dº	Dalzell, Robert	Captain	Major
- - Dº	Hull, James Watson	Captain	No longer in the Service
- - Dº	Wells, Joseph	Major Comg	Lt Colonel
- - Dº	Madden, Windham	Lieutenant	Lieutenant
- - Dº	Freer, William	Lieutenant	Captain
- - Dº	Fergusson, James	Captain	Lt Colonel
- - Dº	Brock, Saumarez	Captain	Major
- - Dº	Mair, Alexander	Lieutenant	Colonel
- - Dº	Lalor, Thomas	Lieutenant	Lieutenant
- - Dº	D'Arcey, Edward	Lieutenant	Captain
- - Dº	Dº - Dº	Dº	
- - Dº	Considine, James	Lieutenant	Lieutenant
44th Dº	Gregory, Edward	Lieutenant	Lt Colonel
- - Dº	Sinclair, Temple Frederick	Lieutenant	Lieutenant
45th Dº	Phillips, Hill	Lieutenant	Lieutenant
- - Dº	Greenwell, Leonard	Major	Lt Colonel
- - Dº	Powell, Francis	Captain	Captain
- - Dº	Martin, Alexander	Captain	Captain
- - Dº	Edmonds, John	Ensign	Lieutenant
- - Dº	Stewart, Ralph Smith	Lieutenant	Lieutenant
- - Dº	Cosby, Philip Stopford	Lieutenant	Lieutenant
- - Dº	Coghlan, James	Lieutenant	Lieutenant
47th Dº	Oglander, Henry	Captain	Lt Colonel
- - Dº	Dº - - Dº	Dº	Dº
- - Dº	Butler, Robert	Lieutenant	Lieutenant
- - Dº	Dº - Dº	Dº	Dº
48th Dº	Erskine, James	Lt Colonel	Lt Colonel
- - Dº	Brooke, John	Lieutenant	Lieutenant
- - Dº	Johnston, James	Lieutenant	Captain
- - Dº	Vincent, Edward	Lieutenant	Lieutenant
- - Dº	Le Mesurier, Henry	Ensign	Lieutenant
- - Dº	Drought, Bartholomew Elliott	Captain	Captain
- - Dº	Johnson, Samuel	Ensign	Lieutenant
- - Dº	Brooke, William	Major Commanding	No longer in the Service
- - Dº	Skeene, George Harwood	Adjutant	Adjutant
- - Dº	Cuthbertson, John	Lieutenant	Lieutenant
- - Dº	Pountney, Henry James	Lieutenant	Lieutenant
- - Dº	Elwood, Charles William	Lieutenant	Lieutenant
- - Dº	Allman, Francis	Captain	Captain
- - Dº	Morrisset, James	Captain	Captain
- - Dº	Robinson, Henry Edward	Lieutenant	Lieutenant
- - Dº	Wilson, Sir James	Lieutenant	Bt Lt Colonel
49th Dº	Hill, William	Ensign	Captain
- - Dº	Robins, William	Captain	Captain
- - Dº	Fitzgerald, Augustine	Captain	Major
- - Dº	Bethune (late Sharpe), Alexander	Captain	Lt Colonel
- - Dº	Lamont, Thomas	Lieutenant	Lieutenant
- - Dº	Clerk, Alexander	Major	Major
50th Dº	Haven, John Gordon	Major	No longer in the Service
- - Dº	McCarthy, I. E. C.	Lieutenant	Captain

PENSIONS FOR THE LOSS OF LIMBS, &c.

Nature of the Cases.	PLACES WHERE, And year when Wounded.		Amount.	Date of Commencement.	
for wounds	Corunna	1809	100	25th December	1811.
for wounds	Burgos	1812	*200	20th September	1813.
for wounds	St. Jean de Luz	1813	100	11th November	1814.
for wounds	St. Jean de Luz	1813	*70	11th November	1814.
loss of a hand	Egypt	1801	200	25th December	1811.
for wounds	Egypt	1801	300	25th December	1811.
loss of an arm	Toulouse	1814	70	11th April	1815.
for wounds	Burgos / Toulouse	1812 / 1814	*70	11th April	1815.
for wounds	Toulouse	1814	*70	11th April	1815.
for a wound	Toulouse	1814	*70	11th April	1815.
ruptured on service	Toulouse	1814	50	11th April	1815.
for wounds	Quatre Bras	1815	*200	17th June	1816.
for a wound	Toulouse	1814	*70	11th April	1815.
loss of a leg	Portugal	1810	100	25th December	1811.
loss of the use of an arm	Portugal	1811	*100	3d April	1812.
for wounds	Coa	1810	*100	25th December	1811.
for wounds	Badajos	1812	*250	8th April	1813.
for wounds	Badajos	1812	*70	7th April	1813.
loss of an arm	Badajos	1812	100	7th April	1813.
for wounds	Ciudad Rodrigo	1812	*100	20th January	1813.
for wounds	Vimeira	1808	*100	25th December	1811.
for wounds	America	1776	100	25th December	1811.
loss of an eye	Spain	1809	70	25th December	1811.
loss of both legs	New Orleans / Do	1795 / —	100 / 100	9th January / Ditto	1816. / —
for wounds	Badajos / and Nivelle	1812 / 1813	*70	11th November	1814.
for wounds	St. Lucia	1796	*300	25th December	1811.
for wounds	Badajos	1812	*70	7th April	1813.
for wounds	Ciudad Rodrigo	1812	*70	20th January	1813.
for wounds	Salamanca	1812	*200	23d July	1813.
for wounds	Badajos	1812	100	7th April	1813.
for wounds	Ciudad Rodrigo	1812	100	20th January	1812.
for wounds	Toulouse	1814	*70	11th April	1815.
for wounds	Orthes	1814	70	28th February	1815.
for wounds	Orthes	1814	*70	28th February	1815.
for a wound	Orthes	1814	70	28th February	1815.
loss of an arm	Badajos	1812	300	7th April	1813.
for other wounds	St. Sebastian	1813	150	1st September	1814.
for wounds	Bidassoa	1812	70	8th October	1814.
injury sustained on service	Do	—	*70	25th December	1815.
for wounds	Badajos	1812	300	7th April	1813.
for wounds	Badajos	1812	70	8th April	1813.
for wounds	Talavera	1809	*70	25th December	1811.
for wounds	Salamanca	1812	70	23d July	1813.
loss of an arm	Salamanca	1812	70	23d July	1813.
for wounds	Albuera	1811	100	17th May	1812.
for wounds	Badajos	1812	50	7th April	1813.
for wounds	Albuera	1811	300	17th May	1812.
loss of a leg	Toulouse	1814	70	11th April	1815.
for wounds	Pampeluna	1813	70	29th July	1814.
for wounds	Pampeluna	1813	*70	29th July	1814.
for wounds	Albuera	1811	*70	17th May	1812.
for wounds	Albuera	1811	*100	17th May	1812.
for wounds	Albuera	1811	100	17th May	1812.
for wounds	Pampeluna	1813	*70	29th July	1814.
for wounds	Albuera / Badajos / Pampeluna / Toulouse	1811 / 1812 / 1813 / 1814	*250	29th July	1814.
loss of an arm	Holland	1799	100	25th December	1811.
for wounds	Holland	1799	100	25th December	1811.
loss of a leg	America	1813	200	25th August	1814.
for wounds	Copenhagen	1801	*100	25th December	1811.
for wounds	America	1812	*70	29th November	1813.
for wounds	Upper Canada	1813	*200	7th June	1814.
loss of an eye	Egypt	1801	200	25th December	1811.
for wounds	Badajos	1812	100	7th April	1813.

(continued)

REGIMENTS.	NAMES.	Rank when Wounded.	Present Rank.
50th Foot	Grant, Charles	Captain	Captain
- - Do	Hill, Charles	Lt Colonel	Lt Colonel
- - Do	Napier, Charles J.	Major Commanding	Lt Colonel
- - Do	Sawkins, William	Lieutenant	Lieutenant
- - Do	Patterson, John	Lieutenant	Lieutenant
- - Do	Turner, William	Lieutenant	Lieutenant
- - Do	Hemsworth, William John	Lieutenant	Lieutenant
- - Do	Brown, Charles,	Lieutenant	Lieutenant
- - Do	Plunkett, Patrick	Lieutenant	Lieutenant
- - Do	Henderson, John William	Captain	Captain
- - Do	Tobin, John	Assistant Surgeon	Ass^t Surg^n in 9th Light Dragoons
- - Do	Custance, Holman	Captain	Captain
51st Do	Roberts, David	Captain	No longer in the Service
- - Do	- - Do	Major	No longer in the Service
- - Do	Hickie, Bartholomew	Lieutenant	Captain
- - Do	Bayly, Henry	Lieutenant	Captain
- - Do	Knollis, Honourable Samuel	Lieutenant	No longer in the Service
- - Do	Kelly, Edward	Captain	Captain
52d Do	Caldwell, Clark	Lieutenant	Major
- - Do	Napier, George Thomas	Major Commanding	Lt Colonel
- - Do	Gibbs, Edward	Lt Colonel	Lt Colonel
- - Do	Campbell, Robert	Captain	Major
- - Do	Mein, William	Lt Colonel	Lt Colonel
- - Do	Love, Frederick William	Ensign	Lieutenant
- - Do	Temple, William Henry	Captain	Captain
- - Do	Nixon, William Richmond	Ensign	Lieutenant
- - Do	Barlow, George Ulrick	Lieutenant	Captn Half-pay 69th Foot
- - Do	Diggle, Charles	B^t Major	B^t Major
- - Do	Anderson, Matthew	Lieutenant	Lieutenant
53d Do	Mansell, Robert Christopher	Captain	Captain
54th Do	Strutt, William Gooday	Brigadier General	Major General
- - Do	- - Do	- - Do	- - Do
- - Do	Digby, Thomas	Major	No longer in the Service
55th Do	Rainey, Henry	Major in the Portuguese service	B^t Major
56th Do	King, Honourable Henry	Captain	Colonel
- - Do	Hadfield, John	Captain	Captain
- - Do	Mallet, John William	Lieutenant	Lt Colonel
- - Do	Owen, Robert	Captain	Major Half-pay 5th Garrison Battalion
57th Do	Shadforth, Thomas	Captain	Major
- - Do	Paterson, Leeson	Lieutenant	Lieutenant
- - Do	Inglis, Sir William	Lt Colonel	Major General
- - Do	Burrows, John	Major	Major
- - Do	McGibbon, Walter	Captain	Major
- - Do	Robinson, And. Delipere	Lieutenant	Lieutenant
- - Do	Leslie, James	Ensign	Lieut^t and Adjut^t
58th Do	Powell, Matthew	Lieutenant	Lieut^t Half-pay 90th F^t
59th Do	Macpherson, Alexander	Captain	Major
- - Do	Crawley, Thomas	Adjutant	Lieutenant
- - Do	Pilkington, Abraham	Captain	Captain
- - Do	Carmichael, Lewis	Lieutenant	Lieutenant
- - Do	Butler, John	Captain	Captain
- - Do	Waters, William Hamilton	Ensign	Lieutenant
- - Do	McPherson, Æneas	Lieutenant	Lieutenant
- - Do	Hoysted, Frederick William	Major	No longer in the Service
- - Do	McPherson, Alexander	Lieutenant	Lieutenant
- - Do	Duncan, Edward	Lieutenant	Captain
60th Do	Livingstone, Alexander	Captain	Captain
- - Do	Broetz, Peter	Adjutant	Lieutenant
- - Do	König, Joseph Von	Lieutenant	Lieutenant
- - Do	Lerche, Gottlieb	Lieutenant	Lieutenant
- - Do	Wynne, Abraham William	Lieutenant	Captain
- - Do	Joyce, John	Lieutenant	Lieutenant
- - Do	Wolff, John Anthony	Captain	Captain
- - Do	Martin, Christopher Bernard	Ensign	Lieutenant

PENSIONS FOR THE LOSS OF LIMBS, &c.

Nature of the Cases.	PLACES WHERE, And year when Wounded.		Amount.	Date of Commencement.	
loss of a leg	Pyrenees	1813	100	26th July	1814.
for wounds	Pyrenees	1813	* 300	26th July	1814.
for wounds {	Corunna	1809	300	25th December	1811.
	Busaco	1810			
loss of a leg	Toulouse	1814	70	11th April	1815.
for wounds	Pyrenees	1813	* 70	26th July	1814.
loss of an hand	Vittoria	1813	70	22d June	1814.
for wounds	Almarez	1812	* 70	20th May	1813.
for wounds	St. Palais	1814	* 70	18th February	1815.
for wounds	Bayonne	1813	* 70	14th December	1814.
for wounds	Toulouse	1814	* 100	3d March	1815.
injury sustained in the performance of military duty	Pyrenees	1813	* 50	23d August	1814.
for wounds	Bayonne	1813	* 100	14th December	1814.
loss of an hand	Lugo	1809	300	25th December	1811.
for wounds	Pyrenees	1813	* 200	1st September	1814.
loss of an arm	Valladolid	1812	100	30th October	1813.
loss of an arm	Lazaca	1813	100	1st September	1814.
for a wound	Minden	1759	70	25th December	1811.
for wounds	St. Sebastian	1813	100	1st September	1814.
loss of an eye	Ceylon	1797	200	25th December	1811.
loss of an arm	Ciudad Rodrigo	1812	300	20th January	1813.
loss of an eye	Badajos	1812	300	7th April	1813.
for wounds	St. Sebastian	1813	200	1st September	1814.
for wounds	Bayonne	1813	300	11th December	1814.
loss of an eye	Antwerp	1814	50	25th September	1815.
for a wound	Nieve	1813	* 100	10th December	1814.
for wounds	Badajos	1812	* 50	26th March	1813.
for a wound	Pyrenees	1813	* 50	11th November	1814.
for a wound	Waterloo	1815	* 200	19th June	1816.
loss of a leg	Waterloo	1815	70	19th June	1816.
for a wound	Toulouse	1814	100	11th April	1815.
loss of a leg	St. Vincent	1796	350	25th December	1811.
for other wounds	Dº	Dº	150	25th December	1811.
loss of an eye	Egypt	1801	200	25th December	1811.
for wounds	Bidart	1813	* 200	11th December	1814.
for wounds	Holland	1790	300	25th December	1811.
for wounds	On board ship	1812	* 100	5th December	1813.
loss of an eye	Holland	1799	300	25th December	1811.
for a wound	Gaudaloupe	1794	* 100	25th December	1811.
for wounds	Albuera	1811	200	17th May	1812.
for wounds	Albuera	1811	* 70	17th May	1812.
for wounds	Albuera	1811	* 300	17th May	1812.
for wounds	Anhoe	1813	* 200	11th November	1814.
for a wound	Albuera	1811	* 100	17th May	1812.
for a wound	Pampeluna	1813	* 70	29th July	1814.
for wounds {	Fort St. Christoval, near Badajos	1811	* 50	10th June	1812.
ruptured on Service	Bourdeaux	1814	70	6th April	1815.
for wounds	Cape of Good Hope	1806	200	25th December	1811.
for wounds	St. Sebastian	1813	* 70	26th July	1814.
for wounds	St. Sebastian	1813	* 100	1st September	1814.
for wounds	Bayonne	1813	70	10th December	1814.
for wounds	Fort Cornelis	1811	* 100	28th August	1812.
for wounds	Fort Cornelis	1811	50	28th August	1812.
for wounds	Bayonne	1813	* 70	12th December	1814.
for wounds	Bayonne	1813	* 250	11th December	1814.
for a wound	Vittoria	1813	* 70	22d June	1814.
for a wound	St. Sebastian	1813	* 70	1st September	1814.
for wounds	Ciudad Rodrigo	1812	100	20th January	1813.
loss of a leg	Badajos	1812	70	7th April	1813.
for a wound	Saints	1809	70	25th December	1811.
loss of an arm	St. Palais	1814	70	16th February	1815.
for a wound	Fuentes D'Honore	1811	70	6th May	1812.
for wounds	Pyrenees	1813	100	26th July	1814.
for wounds	Talavera	1809	* 100	25th December	1811.
for wounds	Pyrenees	1813	* 70	27th July	1814.

(continued)

REGIMENTS.	NAMES.	Rank when Wounded.	Present Rank.
60th Foot	Kelly, Robert	Captain	Captain
- - D°	Harrison, John William	Captain	Major
- - D°	- - - D°	D°	- D°
- - D°	- - - D°	- D°	- D°
- - D°	Purdon, Edward	Captain	Major
- - D°	Tonson, Jacob	Lieutenant	Captain in 84th Foot
- - D°	Zühlcke, George Henry	Lieutenant	B^t Lt Colonel
61st D°	Collins, Graves Chamney	Lieutenant	Captain
- - D°	Stewart, Gilbert	Lieutenant	Captain
- - D°	- - D°	- D°	- D°
- - D°	Daniel, Holland	Lieutenant	Captain
- - D°	Given, James	Lieutenant	Captain
- - D°	Royal, John	Lieutenant	Captain
- - D°	- - D°	- - D°	- D°
- - D°	Collis, John	Lieutenant	Lieutenant
- - D°	- - D°	- - D°	
- - D°	Owen, John	Captain	Major
- - D°	Brackenbury, William	Lieutenant	Major
- - D°	Chapman, James	Lieutenant	Lieutenant
- - D°	Godfrey, Luke	Lieutenant	No longer in the service
- - D°	Singleton, John	Ensign	Lieutenant
- - D°	Falkiner, Samuel	Lieutenant	Lieutenant
- - D°	Bace, William	Adjutant	Lieutenant
- - D°	Eccles, Hugh	Captain	Captain
- - D°	Annesley, Marcus	Captain	Captain
- - D°	White, William	Lieutenant	Lieutenant
- - D°	Greene, William	Captain	Major
- - D°	Bartlet, Spry	Ensign	Lieutenant
- - D°	Langton, Algernon	Brevet Major	B^t Maj. Half-pay 8th F^t
- - D°	Oke, John	Major	B^t Lt Colonel
- - D°	Bace, William	Lieutenant	Lieutenant
62d D°	Oldham, John Field	Captain	Major
- - D°	Shearman, John	Lieutenant	Captain in 13th Foot
63d D°	Wardlaw, Sir John	Lt Colonel	Colonel
- - D°	Lynch, John Blake	Brevet Major	B^t Major
64th D°	Forbes, Anthony Von Som.	Lieutenant	Lieutenant
66th D°	Murray, James P.	Major	Lt Colonel
- - D°	Stephens, W. H.	Captain	Captain
- - D°	Morris, Apollos	Lieutenant	Lieutenant
- - D°	Nicholls, George	Captain	Captain
- - D°	Hay, James	Ensign	Lieutenant
- - D°	Bulstrode, Augustus	Captain	Captain
- - D°	- D° - - D°	- D°	- D°
- - D°	Ferns, William	Captain	Captain
- - D°	Goldie, George Leigh	Major Com^g	B^t Major
67th D°	O'Connell, John	Lieutenant	Lieutenant
68th D°	Thompson, Richard	Major	No longer in the service
- - D°	Mackay, William	Captain	Captain
- - D°	Clarke, Robert	Lieutenant	Lieutenant
- - D°	Johnston, William	Lt Colonel	Colonel
- - D°	Skene, David James	Lieutenant	Lieutenant
- - D°	Stretton, Sev. Wm. Lynam	Ensign	Lieutenant
- - D°	Gough, William	Captain	B^t Major
69th D°	Mitchell, Thomas P.	Captain	Captain
- - D°	Maclachlan, Archibald	Captain	Major
- - D°	Clarke, Charles Christopher	Volunteer	Ensign in 42d Foot
- - D°	Anderson, Henry	Lieutenant	Lieutenant
- - D°	Lindsay, Henry	Captain	B^t Major
- - D°	Hodder, Edward	Lieutenant	Lieutenant
- - D°	Cary, Robert	Captain	Captain, Half-Pay Bourbon Regiment
- - D°	McPherson, Duncan	Lieutenant	Captain in 11th Foot
71st D°	Le Blanc, Henry	Major	Lt Colonel
- - D°	McAlpin, Robert	Acting Adjutant	Lieutenant
- - D°	Brown, James	Captain	No longer in the service
- - D°	Cameron, Donald	Lieutenant	Lieutenant
- - D°	Spottiswoode, George	Captain	Major
- - D°	Lind, Robert	Lieutenant	Lieutenant

PENSIONS FOR THE LOSS OF LIMBS, &c.

Nature of the Cases.	PLACES WHERE, And what year Wounded.		Amount. £.	Date of Commencement.	
for wounds	Tarbes	1814	*100	20th March	1815.
loss of both eyes	Bayonne	1814	200	28th February	1815.
	- D° -	D°	200	- - D°.	
loss of smell and taste	- D° -	D°	100	- - D°.	
for wounds	Toulouse	1814	*100	11th April	1815.
for a wound	St. Vincent	1795	*70	25th December	1811.
for a wound	Talavera	1809	70	25th December	1811.
loss of an arm	Talavera	1809	100	25th December	1811.
loss of an eye	Burgos	1812	100	23d September	1813.
for other wounds	- D° -	D°	100	- - D°	- - D°
for a wound	Salamanca	1812	100	23d July	1813.
for a wound	Talavera	1809	*70	25th December	1811.
loss of a leg	Salamanca	1812	100	23d July	1813.
loss of the use of an arm	Salamanca	1812	100	23d July	1813.
loss of both eyes	Salamanca	1812	70	23d July	1813.
	- D° -	D°	70	- D° -	D°.
loss of an arm	Salamanca	1812	200	24th June	1813.
for wounds	Salamanca	1812	70	23d July	1813.
for wounds	Salamanca	1812	70	23d July	1813.
loss of an eye	Egypt	1801	200	25th December	1811.
for a wound	Salamanca	1812	*50	23d July	1813.
for a wound	Salamanca	1812	*70	23d July	1813.
loss of an eye	-	1812	70	25th December	1813.
for a wound	Bayonne	1813	*100	11th November	1814.
for a wound	St. Pè	1813	*70	11th November	1814.
for wounds	Toulouse	1814	*70	11th April	1815.
for wounds	Toulouse	1814	*100	11th April	1815.
for wounds	Toulouse	1814	*50	11th April	1815.
for a wound	Quatre Bras	1815	*200	17th June	1816.
for wounds	Toulouse	1814	*200	11th April	1815.
rupture and other injury	-	1813 and 1814	70	25th December	1816.
for wounds	Palinura	1811	200	1st November	1812.
for wounds	St. Vincent	1812	*100	9th October	1813.
for wounds	Egmont-op-Zee	1799	300	25th December	1811.
for a wound	Guadaloupe	1815	200	10th August	1816.
loss of an eye	France	1815	70	25th December	1816.
for a wound	Douro	1809	300	25th December	1811.
for wounds	Talavera	1809	100	25th December	1811.
for wounds	Talavera	1809	*70	25th December	1811.
for wounds	Vittoria	1813	*100	22d June	1814.
for wounds	Albuera	1811	*70	17th May	1812.
for wounds	Bayonne	1813	100	14th December	1814.
- D° -	- D° -	D°	100	- - D° -	D°.
for wounds	Albuera	1811	100	17th May	1812.
for wounds	Pyrenees	1813	*250	30th July	1814.
loss of an arm	Pampeluna	1813	70	31st July	1814.
loss of an arm	Flushing	1809	300	25th December	1811.
for wounds	Salamanca	1812	100	22d June	1813.
loss of a leg	St. Pè	1813	100	11th November	1814.
for wounds	Vittoria	1813	*300	22d June	1814.
for wounds	Vera	1813	70	1st September	1814.
for wounds	Vittoria	1813	*50	22d June	1814.
for a wound	Vittoria	1813	*100	22d June	1814.
for wounds	Java	1811	100	24th August	1812.
for wounds	Vellore	1806	*200	25th December	1811.
for wounds	Quatre Bras	1815	*50	17th June	1816.
for a wound	Waterloo	1815	*70	19th June	1816.
for wounds	Quatre Bras	1815	*100	17th June	1816.
for a wound	Waterloo	1815	*70	19th June	1816.
for a wound	Bergen-op-Zoom	1814	*100	9th March	1815.
for a wound	Java	1811	*70	27th August	1812.
loss of a leg	Buenos Ayres	1806	300	25th December	1811.
loss of the use of an arm	Vimiera	1808	70	25th December	1811.
for a wound	Helder	1799	100	25th December	1811.
for wounds	America	1782	70	25th December	1811.
for wounds	Badajos	1812	*200	7th April	1813.
for a wound	Waterloo	1815	*70	19th June	1816.

(continued)

REGIMENTS.	NAMES.	Rank when Wounded.	Present Rank.
71st Foot	Cadogan, Honourable Edward	Captain	Major, Half-Pay 8th West India Regim^t
73d D°	M'Donald, James	Major	No longer in the service
- - D°	Fraser, John	Lieutenant	Lt General
- - D°	Riach, John	Ass^t Surgeon	Ass^t Surgeon
- - D°	Garland, John	Captain	Captain
- - D°	McLeod, William	Captain	Sold out
74th D°	Moore, Norman John	Captain	No longer in the service
- - D°	Lister, Thomas St. George	Lieutenant	Captain
- - D°	Longlands, George	Captain	Major
- - D°	White, Henry	Adjutant	Lieutenant
- - D°	Duncombe, Francis	Lieutenant	Lieutenant
- - D°	Pattison, Alexander Hope	Lieutenant	Lieutenant
- - D°	Alves, John	Lieutenant	Lieutenant
- - D°	Lister, Thomas St. George	Captain	Captain
- - D°	Mac Queen, Donald	Captain	Captain
75th D°	Mackay, Donald	Lieutenant	Lt Colonel
76th D°	Crossgrove, William	Lieutenant	Paymaster
- - D°	McDonald, Alexander	Brevet Major	Major
77th D°	Maclaine, Murdoch Hugh	Captain	Major
- - D°	Browne, Andrew Valentine	Captain	Major
- - D°	- - D° - - D°	- D°	D°
- - D°	Lawrence, Alexander	Lieutenant	Lt Colonel
- - D°	Clerke, John Augustus	Lieutenant	Lieutenant
78th D°	Christie, Archibald	Lieutenant	Colonel
- - D°	- - D° - - D°	- - D°	- D°
- - D°	Munro, Hugh	Captain	No longer in the service
- - D°	- D° - - D°	- D°	
- - D°	Stewart, David	Major Com^g	Colonel
- - D°	Macleod, John	Lt Colonel	Colonel
- - D°	Sinclair, George	Ensign	Ensign
- - D°	Mackenzie, William	Captain	Captain
- - D°	Forbes, David	Lieutenant	Lt Colonel
79th D°	Brown, Charles	Lieutenant	Lieutenant
- - D°	Douglas, Neil	Captain	Lt Colonel
- - D°	Webb, John W.	Lieutenant	Captain
- - D°	Egan, Michael	Surgeon	Apothecary
- - D°	- D° -	- D°	- D°
- - D°	Cameron, Ewen	Lieutenant	Lieutenant
- - D°	Travers, Robert	Colonel	Colonel
- - D°	Marshall, William	Captain	Captain
- - D°	Maddock, William	Lieutenant	Captain
- - D°	Brown, Thomas	Captain	Captain
- - D°	Brown, Andrew	Major	B^t Lt Colonel
80th Foot	Paget, Sir Edward	Lt General	Lt General
- - D°	Trant, William	Lieutenant	Lieutenant
81st D°	Chislett, Henry	Assistant Surgeon	Assistant Surgeon
- - D°	Hort, Josiah G.	Lieutenant	Captain
- - D°	Milling, Henry	Major	Lt Colonel
- - D°	Colclough, Cesar	Captain	Captain
- - D°	D° D°	D°	D°
82d D°	Hastings, Charles Holland	Captain	Lt Colonel
- - D°	Agnew, Thomas Ramsden	Lieutenant	Captain
- - D°	Fitzgerald, W. E.	Major	Major
- - D°	Goslett, Joseph	Quarter Master	Lieutenant
- - D°	Grant, William	Lt Colonel	M. General
- - D°	Derenzy, George Webb	Lieutenant	Captain
- - D°	Mason, Edward Ussher	Ensign	Lieutenant
- - D°	Conyers, Charles Edward	Major Com^g	Lt Colonel
- - D°	Boyd, John	Lieutenant	Captain
- - D°	Latham, Robert J.	Lieutenant	Lieutenant
- - D°	Pratt, Charles	Lieutenant	Major Half pay 96th Foot
83d D°	Matthews, Joseph	Lieutenant	Lieutenant
- - D°	Nicholson, John	Lieutenant	Captain
- - D°	Bowles, Charles Proby	Lieutenant	Lieutenant
- - D°	Baldwin, Connel James	Lieutenant	Lieutenant
- - D°	Wyatt, Herbert	Lieutenant	Lieutenant
- - D°	Lane, Ambrose	Lieutenant	Lieutenant

Nature of the Cases.	PLACES WHERE, And year when Wounded.		Amount.	Date of Commencement.	
health impaired on service	–	–	*200	25th December	1815.
for wounds	India	1801	200	25th December	1811.
loss of a leg	Gibraltar	1782	400	25th December	1811.
impaired vision, in consequence of ophthalmia	–	1814	50	25th January	1815.
for a wound	Waterloo	1815	100	19th June	1816.
for a wound	Seringapatam	1799	100	25th December	1811.
for wounds	Assaye	1803	100	25th December	1811.
for wounds	Badajos	1812	*70	27th March	1813.
for wounds	Badajos	1812	*200	7th April	1813.
for wounds	Vittoria	1813	70	22d June	1814.
for wounds	Pyrenees	1813	70	31st July	1814.
for wounds	Pampeluna	1813	70	1st August	1814.
loss of an eye	Spain	1812	70	25th December	1813.
for wounds	Orthes	1814	*100 2d Pension	28th February	1815.
for a wound	Toulouse	1814	*100	11th April	1815.
loss of the use of a knee	East Indies	1800	300	25th December	1811.
for wounds	Bhurtpore	1805	70	25th December	1811.
for wounds	Delhi	1803	*100	25th December	1811.
loss of a leg	Cuidad Rodrigo	1812	200	20th January	1813.
loss of a leg	Walcheren	1809	200	25th December	1811.
loss of the use of a hand	- D° -	D°	100	- - D°	D°.
for wounds	Seringapatam	1799	100	25th December	1811.
for wounds	Badajos	1812	*70	7th April	1813.
loss of an eye	Holland	1794	300	25th December	1811
for other injury	- D° -	D°	300	- - D°	D°.
loss of both eyes	Nimeguen	1794	100	25th December	1811.
	- D° -	D°	100	- - D°	D°.
for wounds	Maida	1806	250	25th December	1811.
for a wound	Merxem	1814	*300	14th January	1815.
for a wound	Merxem	1814	*50	3d February	1815.
for a wound	Java	1811	*100	27th August	1812.
loss of an eye	Bengal	1798	300	25th December	1811.
loss of a leg	Fuentes d'Honore	1811	70	4th May	1812.
for a wound	Busaco	1810	*300	25th December	1811.
for wounds	Salamanca	1812	100	23d July	1813.
loss of an eye	Egypt	1801	100	25th December	1811.
for wounds	- D° -	D°	100	- - D°	D°.
for wounds	Toulouse	1814	*70	11th April	1815.
loss of an eye	Ferrol	1800	300	25th December	1811.
loss of an arm	Quatre Bras	1815	100	17th June	1816.
for a wound	Quatre Bras	1815	*70	17th June	1816.
for a wound	Quatre Bras	1815	*100	17th June	1816.
for a wound	Quatre Bras	1815	*200	17th June	1816.
loss of an arm	Portugal	1809	400	25th December	1811.
loss of a leg	India	1811	70	24th June	1812.
loss of a leg	Flushing	1809	50	25th December	1811.
loss of a leg	Corunna	1809	100	25th December	1811.
for a wound	Corunna	1809	*300	25th December	1811.
injury sustained in the performance of military duty	Ireland	1806	100	25th December	1811.
	D°	—	100	- - D°	D°
loss of an arm	Copenhagen	1807	300	25th December	1811.
loss of a leg	Vittoria	1813	100	22d June	1814.
for wounds	Pampeluna	1813	200	31st July	1814.
injury sustained in the performance of military duty	Spain	1812	50	25th December	1813.
for wounds	Vittoria	1813	300	22d June	1814.
loss of an arm	Vittoria	1813	100	22d June	1814.
for a wound	Pyrenees	1813	50	31st July	1814.
for wounds	Orthes	1814	*250	28th February	1815.
for a wound	Pyrences	1813	*70	31st July	1814.
for a wound	Fort Erie	1814	*70	18th September	1815.
for a wound	Flushing	1809	*200	25th December	1811.
Loss of an arm	Ciudad Rodrigo	1812	70	13th January	1813.
loss of a leg	Talavera	1809	100	25th December	1811.
for wounds	Badajos	1812	*100	7th April	1813.
for a wound	Talavera	1809	*70	25th December	1811.
for wounds	Nivelle	1813	*70	11th November	1814.
for a wound	Badajos	1812	*50	7th April	1813.

(continued.)

REGIMENTS.	NAMES.	Rank when Wounded.	Present Rank.
84th Dº	Holmes, Joseph	Lieutenant	Lieutenant
85th Dº	Travers, Joseph	Lieutenant	No longer in the Service
- - Dº	Brown, George	Major	Lᵗ Colonel
- - Dº	Crouchley, Thomas	Lieutenant	Lieutenant
- - Dº	Gascoyne, Frederick	Lieutenant	Captain Half-pay 3d Garrⁿ Batt.
86th Dº	Home, William	Lieutenant	Lieutenant
- - Dº	Paton, Robert	Ensign	Ensign
87th Dº	Rose, Alexander	Captain	Major
- - Dº	Bagenall, John Doyle	Lieutenant	Lieutenant
- - Dº	Barton, James Campbell	Lieutenant	Captain
- - Dº	Gough, Hugh	Major Comᵍ	Lᵗ Colonel
- - Dº	King, James	Captain	Captain
- - Dº	Kelly, John	Lieutenant	Lieutenant
- - Dº	Bagenall, Robert Sedley	Ensign	Ensign
- - Dº	Mountgarret, William	Lieutenant	Lieutenant
- - Dº	Hooper, Henry	Brevet Lᵗ Colonel	Lᵗ Colonel
- - Dº	Maclane, Archibald	Major	Lᵗ Colonel Half-pay 7th West India Regᵗ
- - Dº	Bourne, Wm. Henry	Volunteer	Lieutenant Half-pay 21st Foot
88th Dº	Kingsmill, William	Lieutenant	Lieutenant
- - Dº	Nickle, William	Lieutenant	Captain
- - Dº	Flack, William	Lieutenant	Captain
- - Dº	Fitzpatrick, John	Lieutenant	Captain
- - Dº	Dº - Dº	Dº	Dº
- - Dº	Cresswell, George	Lieutenant	Lieutenant
- - Dº	Chisholm, James	Captain	Bᵗ Lᵗ Colonel in African Corps
- - Dº	Oates, James Poole	Captain	Bᵗ Major
- - Dº	Flack, John	Captain	Captain, Half-pay 10th Vetⁿ Batt.
89th Dº	Gray, William	Lieutenant	Lieutenant
- - Dº	Barney, William	Captain	Major
- - Dº	Morrison, Joseph Wanton	Lᵗ Colonel	Lᵗ Colonel
90th Dº	Vigoureux, George	Major	Lᵗ Colonel
- - Dº	Cartwright, William	Lieutenant	Captain
91st Dº	Briggs, James	Ensign	Lieutenant
- - Dº	McNeill, Donald	Major Comᵍ	Lᵗ Colonel
- - Dº	Gunn, William	Captain	Captain
92d Dº	Grant, Peter	Major	Major
- - Dº	Macdonald, Donald	Captain	Lᵗ Colonel
- - Dº	Campbell, Dugald	Captain	Major
- - Dº	Macdonald, Ronald	Captain	Captain
- - Dº	Gordon, George	Lieutenant	Lieutenant
- - Dº	Fraser, George	Lieutenant	Lieutenant
- - Dº	Mackie, George	Lieutenant	Lᵗ and Adjᵗ
- - Dº	Hewitt, Robert	Ensign	Ensign
- - Dº	McKinley, John	Lieutenant	Lieutenant
- - Dº	Ross, Ewan	Lieutenant	Lieutenant
- - Dº	Bramwell, John	Ensign	Lieutenant
- - Dº	Macdonald, Ronald	Lieutenant	Lieutenant
- - Dº	Macdonald, Donald	Lieutenant	Lieutenant
93d Dº	Scobie, James	Lieutenant	Captain
- - Dº	Hay, James	Lieutenant	Lieutenant
- - Dº	Graves, Wm. Valentine	Lieutenant	Lieutenant
94th Dº	Donald, James	Paymaster	Paymaster
- - Dº	Cooke, James	Captain	Captain
- - Dº	Fraser, Andrew	Captain	Captain
- - Dº	Cairncross, Alexander	Captain	Captain
- - Dº	McArthur, Archibald	Lieutenant	Captain
- - Dº	Taylor, Arthur Sanders	Lieutenant	Captain
- - Dº	Thornton, John	Lieutenant	Lieutenant

PENSIONS FOR THE LOSS OF LIMBS, &c.

Nature of the Cases.	PLACES WHERE, And year when Wounded.		Amount.	Date of Commencement.	
for a wound	Bayonne	1813	*70	11th December	1814.
for wounds	Helder	1799	70	25th December	1811.
for a wound	Bladensburgh	1814	*200	25th August	1813.
for a wound	Bladensburgh	1814	*70	25th August	1815.
for a wound	Bladensburgh	1814	*70	25th August	1815.
for wounds	Bourbon	1810	70	25th December	1811.
loss of an eye	Egypt	1801	50	25th December	1811.
loss of an eye	Buenos Ayres	1807	200	25th December	1811.
loss of an arm	Talavera	1809	100	25th December	1811.
for wounds	Barrosa	1811	*100	6th March	1812.
for wounds	Talavera	1809	300	25th December	1811.
for wounds	Vittoria	1813	*100	22d June	1814.
loss of a leg	St. Pe	1813	70	11th November	1814.
for a wound	St. Pe	1813	50	11th December	1814.
for wounds	Egypt / Vittoria / Orthes	1807 / 1813 / 1814	70	28th February	1815.
loss of a leg	New Orleans	1804	300	25th December	1815.
for wounds	Barrosa	1811	*200	6th March	1812.
for a wound	St. Pe	1813	*70	11th November	1813.
loss of a leg	Ciudad Rodrigo	1812	70	20th January	1813.
loss of a leg	Salamanca	1812	100	23d July	1813.
for wounds	Ciudad Rodrigo	1812	100	17th January	1813.
for wounds	Busaco	1810	100	25th December	1811.
loss of an eye	Orthes	1814	100	28th February	1815.
for a wound	Orthes	1814	70	28th February	1815.
for wounds	Doig / Buenos Ayres	1804 / 1807	300	25th December	1811.
for wounds	St. Domingo / Cape St. Nicola / Talavera / Badajos / Orthes	1794 / 1795 / 1809 / 1812 / 1814	100	25th June	1816.
loss of an eye	Ireland	1802	100	25th December	1811.
for a wound	Canada	1814	*70	26th July	1815.
for a wound	Fort Erie	1814	*100	16th August	1815.
for a wound	Niagara	1814	*300	26th July	1815.
loss of the use of a leg	Egypt	1801	300	25th December	1811.
for a wound	Egypt	1801	100	25th December	1811.
for a wound	Bergen-op-zoom	1814	*50	9th March	1815.
for a wound	Pyrenees	1813	*300	31st July	1814.
for a wound	Orthes	1814	*100	28th February	1815.
loss of a leg	Villa Formosa	1811	200	5th May	1812.
for wounds	Arroyo de Molinos	1811	300	29th October	1812.
for wounds	Pampeluna	1813	200	1st August	1814.
for wounds	Bayonne	1813	100	14th December	1814.
for wounds	Pampeluna	1813	*70	26th July	1814.
for a wound	Holland	1799	70	25th December	1811.
for wounds	Quatre Bras	1815	*70	17th June	1816.
loss of a leg	Quatre Bras	1815	50	17th June	1816.
for a wound	Quatre Bras	1815	*70	17th June	1816.
for a wound	Quatre Bras	1815	*70	17th June	1816.
for a wound	Quatre Bras	1815	*70	17th June	1816.
for a wound	Quatre Bras	1815	*70	17th June	1816.
for a wound	Waterloo	1815	*70	19th June	1816.
for wounds	Cape of Good Hope	1806	70	25th December	1811.
loss of an eye	New Orleans	1815	70	9th January	1816.
for a wound	New Orleans	1815	*70	9th January	1816.
for a wound	Argaum	1803	100	25th December	1811.
for a wound	Salamanca	1812	100	23d July	1813.
loss of sight	East Indies	1807	100	25th December	1811.
for wounds	Vittoria	1813	100	22d June	1814.
for wounds	Vittoria	1813	100	22d June	1814.
for wounds	Ciudad Rodrigo	1812	100	20th January	1813.
for wounds	Sara	1813	*70	11th November	1814.

(continued)

REGIMENTS.	NAMES.	Rank when Wounded.	Present Rank.
94th Foot	Tweedie James	Lieutenant	Lieutenant, Half-pay 7th Foot
95th Foot (late 96th D°)	Lamb, Thomas	Lieutenant	Captain
96th D° (late 97th D°)	Sutton, Matthew	Major of Brigade	No longer in the Service
- - D°	D° - D°	D°	
- - D°	Coppinger, Thomas G.	Captain	Captain
99th D° (late 100th D°)	Fawcett, Richard Vyse	Captain	Major
- - D°	Sleigh, William	Captain	Captain
- - D°	Sherrard, Thomas Ormsby	Captain	Captain
103d D°	Cuppage, Alexander	Lieutenant	Sold out
- - D°	Fallon, John	Lieutenant	Lieutenant
Rifle Brigade (late 95th Foot)	Hope, John Charles	Lieutenant	Lieutenant
- - D°	Percival, William	Captain	Lt Colonel
- - D°	D°	D°	D°
- - D°	Manners, Henry Herbert	Lieutenant	Lieutenant
- - D°	Fensham, Daniel	Lieutenant	Lieutenant
- - D°	M‘Culloch, John Garlies	Lieutenant	Major
- - D°	Campbell, William	Lieutenant	Lieutenant
- - D°	Hamilton, William	Lieutenant	Lieutenant
- - D°	Pemberton, Andrew Wale	Lieutenant	Captain
- - D°	Johnstone, William	Lieutenant	Captain
- - D°	Scott, Henry	Lieutenant	Lieutenant
- - D°	Fitzmaurice, John	2d Lieutenant	Lieutenant
- - D°	Percival, James	Lieutenant	Captain
- - D°	Hart, John Blackburn	Captain	Major
- - D°	Gray, Loftus	Captain	Major
- - D°	Llewellyn, Henry	Lieutenant	Lieutenant
- - D°	Fitzgerald, Richard	2d Lieutenant	Lieutenant
- - D°	Hewan, Michael	Captain	Captain
- - D°	Travers, James	Captain	Captain
- - D°	Barker, Robert	2d Lieutenant	Lieutenant
- - D°	Ribton, Sir John	Lieutenant	Lieutenant
- - D°	Cox, John	Lieutenant	Lieutenant
- - D°	Cameron, Alexander	Lt Colonel	Lt Colonel
- - D°	- - - D°	- D°	- D°
- - D°	Humbley, William	Lieutenant	Captain
- - D°	M‘Cullock, John Garlies	Major	Major, half-pay 2d Garrison Battalion
- - D°	Walsh, John Prendergast	2d Lieutenant	Ensign, half-pay 90th Foot
- - D°	Wilkins, George	Lt Colonel	B^t Lt Colonel
- - D°	Beckwith, Charles	Brevet Lt Colonel	B^t Lt Colonel
- - D°	Norcott, Amos Godsil Robert	Major	B^t Lt Colonel
- - D°	Simmons, George	Lieutenant	Lieutenant
- - D°	Lynam, Joseph	Lieutenant	Lieutenant
3d West India Regiment	Rainsford, Marcus	Captain	No longer in the Service
- - - D°	Gledstanes, Joshua	Captain	Major
6th - D°	Leigh, Charles	Major	Major
7th - D°	Pakenham, Hon. Hercules Robert	Major	Lt Colonel
Royal Waggon Train	Mac Dowal, Joseph	Lieutenant	Lieutenant
York Rangers	Burke, Francis	Lieutenant	B^t Colonel
Glengary Fencibles	Jenkins, John	Captain	Captain
- - - D°	M‘Pherson, Daniel	Captain	Captain
York Hussars	Seelinger, John Joseph	Brevet Major	Major
Canadian Fencibles	Hall, John	Captain	Captain
- - - D°	Robertson, George	Lt Colonel	Lt Colonel
Royal Staff Corps	Hulme, William Brown	Lieutenant	Captain
Nova Scotia Fencibles	Courtenay, John Edward	Brevet Major	B^t Major
7th Veteran Battalion	Macfarlane, James	Lieutenant	Lieutenant

PENSIONS FOR THE LOSS OF LIMBS, &c.

Nature of the Cases.	PLACES WHERE, And year when wounded.		Amount.	Date of Commencement.	
ruptured on service	Badajos	1812	* 70	26th March	1813.
injury sustained in the performance of military duty	Guadaloupe	1810	70	25th December	1811.
loss of the right eye	Egypt	1801	200	25th December	1811.
impaired vision of the left eye	Dº	—	* 100	- - Dº	Dº
for a wound	St. Christoval	1811	* 100	11th May	1812.
for a wound	Canada	1813	* 200	31st December	1814.
for wounds	Canada	1814	100	6th July	1815.
for a wound	Canada	1814	* 100	6th July	1815.
for wounds	Fort Erie	1814	* 70	16th August	1815.
for wounds	Fort Erie	1814	* 70	16th August	1815.
for wounds	Barrosa	1811	70	6th March	1812.
loss of the use of an arm	Sobraul	1810	300	25th December	1811.
for other wounds	Dº	—	100	- - Dº	Dº
for wounds	Badajos	1812	* 70	7th April	1813.
loss of an eye	Navarre	1813	70	11th November	1814.
loss of the use of an arm	Puenta de Marulla	1811	200	16th March	1812.
for wounds	Barrosa	1811	* 70	6th March	1812.
for wounds	St. Sebastian	1813	70	1st September	1814.
for wounds	Pyrenees	1813	100	3d August	1814.
for wounds	Badajos	1812	70	7th April	1813.
for a wound	Bayonne	1813	70	10th November	1814.
for a wound	Badajos	1812	* 50	7th April	1813.
for a wound	St. Sebastian	1813	70	1st September	1814.
for wounds	Vera	1813	100	8th October	1814.
for a wound	Tarbes	1814	* 100	21st March	1815.
for a wound	Pyrenees	1813	70	1st September	1814.
for a wound	Merxem	1814	* 70	3d February	1815.
for a wound	Toulouse	1814	* 100	11th April	1815.
for a wound	New Orleans	1815	* 200	9th January	1816.
for a wound	New Orleans	1815	* 50	9th January	1816.
for a wound	New Orleans	1815	* 70	9th January	1816.
for wounds	Ciudad Rodrigo and Tarbes	1812 1814	* 70	21st March	1815.
for wounds	Waterloo	1815	300	19th June	1816.
- - Dº -	- - Dº -	—	200	25th June	1816.
for a wound	Waterloo	1815	* 70	19th June	1816.
loss of left arm	Waterloo	1815	200	19th June	1816.
loss of a leg	Waterloo	1815	50	19th June	1816.
for a wound	Waterloo	1815	* 300	19th June	1816.
loss of a leg	Waterloo	1815	300	19th June	1816.
for wounds	Tarbes and Waterloo	1814 1815	* 250	19th June	1816.
for wounds	Waterloo	1815	* 70	19th June	1816.
for a wound	Waterloo	1815	* 70	19th June	1816.
injury sustained while a prisoner of war	St. Domingo	1796	100	25th December	1811.
for wounds	Martinique	1809	* 200	25th December	1811.
for a wound	St. Domingo	1796	* 200	25th December	1811.
for a wound	Badajos	1812	* 200	7th April	1813.
loss of the sight of an eye	Spain	1813	70	25th June	1814.
for wounds	Flanders	1794	70	25th December	1811.
loss of an arm	Osdenburgh Canada	1813	100	23d February	1814.
for a wound, and injury sustained in the performance of military duty	Sackett's Harbour London	1813 1815	* 100	30th May	1814.
for a wound	St. Domingo	1797	200	25th December	1811.
injury sustained in the performance of military duty	Canada	1814	* 100	14th October	1815
injury sustained in the performance of military duty	Canada	1814	* 300	25th September	1815.
ruptured on service	Portugal	1808	70	25th December	1816.
injury sustained in the performance of military duty	Quebec	1814	* 200	25th December	1815.
loss of an eye	Gibraltar	1813	70	24th June	1814

(continued)

REGIMENTS.	NAMES.	Rank when Wounded.	Present Rank.
11th ditto	Pettigrew, William	Lieutenant	Lieutenant, 5th Vetⁿ Battⁿ
R^l West India Rangers	Kennedy, William	Captain	Captain
Sicilian Regiment	Strode, James	Ensign	Lieutenant
Queen's Rangers	McCrea, Robert	Captain	Major
- - D°	- - D°	- D°	- D°
1st Veteran Battalion	Mair, Alexander	Lt Colonel	Colonel
British American Legion	Tarleton, Banastre	Lt Colonel	General
- - - D°	Donovan, Jeremiah	Lieutenant	Lieutenant
Late Duke of Cumberland's Regiment	Bramwell, John	Lieutenant	Lieutenant
Late 26th Dragoons	King, Henry	Captain Lieutenant	Lt Colonel
Inspecting Field Officer of Militia in Canada	St. George, Thomas Bligh	Lt Colonel	Colonel
- - - D°	Pearson, Thomas	Lt Colonel	Lt Colonel in 23d Foot
Chasseurs Brittaniques	Eustace, William C.	Lt Colonel	Lt Colonel
- - - D°	Napier, Thomas Erskine	Captain	Lt Colonel
Meuron's Regiment	Herries, William Lewis	Captain	Lt Colonel
Staff	Walker, George Townsend	Major General	Major General
- D°	Waller, Robert	Chief of the Quarter Master Gen^{ls} Staff	Lt Colonel
- D°	Colville, Hon. Sir Charles	Major General	Major General
- D°	Vivian, Sir R. Hussey	Colonel	Major General
- D°	Douglas, Sir James	Colonel	Lt Colonel
- D°	Bradford, Sir Thomas	Major General	Major General
- D°	Cooke, Sir George	Major General	Major General
- D°	Halket, Sir Colin	Major General	Major General
- D°	Coghlan, Edmund	Aide-de-Camp	Lt Colonel, half pay 3d Garrison Batt.
Hospital Staff	Farquharson, Thomas	Deputy Inspector of Hospitals	Surgeon
- - D°	Blicke, W.	Staff Surgeon	Staff Surgeon
- - D°	Redmond, Gabriel Rice	Inspector of Hospitals	Insp^r of Hospitals
- - D°	Hill, John Perkins	Staff Surgeon	Surgeon
- - D°	Quartley, Charles	Staff Surgeon	Surgeon
- - D°	Griffith, Charles	Staff Surgeon	Dep^y Inspector
- - D°	Smyth, Thomas	Deputy Purveyor	Dep^y Purveyor
- - D°	Griffith, Edmund	Purveyor's Clerk	
Volunteer	Collis, William		Major
- D°	Spalding, Warner		Lieutenant
- D°	Perry, Francis		Lieutenant
- D°	Brown, William		Lieutenant
- D°	Holmes, Henry Hayes		Ensign
- D°	Murray, William		Ensign
4th Jersey Militia	Brohier, Lewis Nathaniel John	Lieutenant	Ensign
1st Portuguese Cavalry	Watson, Henry	Lt Colonel	Lt Colonel
1st Portuguese Infantry	Mac Intosh, Robert	Captain	Captain
2d - D°	Ray, Robert	Major	Major
8th - D°	Elder, Sir George	Lt Colonel	Lt Colonel
- - D°	Marley, Edward Stephen	Captain	Lt Colonel
- - D°	Ouseley, Ralph	Lt Colonel	Major
9th D°	Ross, Archibald	Lt Colonel	Major
- - D°	Cotter, William	Captain	Captain
10th D°	Gordon, William	Captain	Captain
12th D°	Thornton, William Henry	Captain	Captain
14th D°	Potter, Thomas	Captain	Captain
- - D°	Macdonald, John	Lt Colonel	Major

PENSIONS FOR THE LOSS OF LIMBS, &C.

Nature of the Cases.	PLACES WHERE, And year when Wounded.	Amount.	Date of Commencement.
loss of an eye	Isle of Man - 1814	70	25th December - 1815.
injury sustained in the performance of military duty	Trinidad - 1813	* 100	24th April - 1814.
loss of hearing	Malta - 1811	50	25th June - 1812.
loss of the use of an arm	Brandywine - 1777	200	25th December - 1811.
for a wound	- - Do - -	100	25th June - 1816.
loss of left arm	Portsea - 1804	2d Pension 300	25th December - 1811.
for wounds	America - 1781	300	25th December - 1811.
for wounds	America - 1780	70	25th December - 1811.
for wounds	On board ship 1781 and 1782	70	25th December - 1811.
loss of a leg	Egypt - 1801	300	25th December - 1811.
for a wound	Fort Erie - 1813	* 300	23d January - 1814.
for wounds	Fort Erie - 1814	300	26th September - 1815.
for a wound	St. Sebastian - 1813	300	1st September - 1814.
loss of an arm	Bayonne - 1813	300	12th December - 1814.
loss of a leg	Bayonne - 1814	300	15th April - 1815.
for wounds	Badajos - 1812	350	7th April - 1813.
for wounds	Albuera - 1811	300	16th May - 1812.
for wounds	Badajos - 1812	* 350	7th April - 1813.
for a wound	Toulouse - 1814	* 350	8th April - 1815.
loss of a leg	Toulouse - 1814	350	11th April - 1815.
for a wound	Bayonne - 1814	350	15th April - 1815.
loss of an arm	Waterloo - 1815	350	19th June - 1816.
for a wound	Waterloo - 1815	350	19th June - 1816.
injury sustained in the performance of military duty	Sicily - 1811	100	10th January - 1812.
loss of an arm	India - 1787	200	25th December - 1811.
loss of an eye	Palermo - 1813	100	16th July - 1814.
injury sustained in the performance of military duty	America - 1812	* 300	25th December - 1813.
loss of an eye	West Indies - 1810	* 100	25th December - 1811.
injury sustained in the performance of military duty	Spain - 1813	100	24th December - 1814.
injury sustained in the performance of military duty	Spike Island - 1796	100	25th December - 1811.
ruptured on service	Portugal - 1809	50	25th December - 1811.
loss of an eye	Sicily - 1814	50	8th November - 1815.
loss of a hand	West Indies - 1793	200	25th December - 1811.
loss of an arm	Holland - 1799	70	25th December - 1811.
loss of an arm	Salamanca - 1812	50	23d July - 1813.
loss of a leg	Germany - 1758	70	25th December - 1811.
loss of a leg	Toulouse - 1814	50	11th April - 1815.
for a wound	Vittoria - 1813	* 50	22d June - 1814.
loss of an arm	Jersey - 1787	70	25th December - 1811.
for a wound	Salamanca - 1812	* 300	23d July - 1813.
loss of an eye	Spain - 1814	100	25th December - 1815.
for wounds	Pampeluna - 1813	200	31st July - 1814.
for wounds	Badajos - 1812	300	7th April - 1813.
for wounds	Salamanca - 1812	100	23d July - 1813.
for wounds	Pyrenees - 1813	300	1st September - 1814.
for a wound	Vittoria - 1813	300	22d June - 1814.
for a wound	Vittoria - 1813	* 200	22d June - 1814.
for wounds	Nivelle - 1813	100	11th November - 1814.
for a wound	Pampeluna - 1813	100	29th July - 1814.
for a wound	Aire - 1814	* 100	3d March - 1815.
for wounds	Bagarre - 1813	* 300	3d October - 1814.

(continued.)

NAMES OF THE OFFICERS IN THE ARMY, WHO RECEIVE

REGIMENTS.	NAMES.	Rank when Wounded.	Present Rank.
23d Portuguese Infantry	O'Neill, Thomas	Captain	Bt Major
3d Caçadores	Dobbin, William	Captain	Captain
4th Do	Armstrong, Frederick	Captain	Captain
Do	McGregor, Alexander	Captain	Captain
7th Do	Hawkshaw, Edward	Major	Lt Colonel
Do	O'Toole, Bryan	Lt Colonel	Lt Colonel
Do	Lillie, Sir John Scot	Major	Major
8th Do	Western, Charles Maximilian Thomas	Captain	Captain
10th Do	Hardcastle, William Augustus	Captain	Ensign
11th Do	De Borgh, Anthony Philip	Captain	Captain
Spanish Service	Downie, Sir John	Brigr General	No Rank in the British Army
Do	Clarke, Sir John	Lt Colonel	Lt Colonel
Inverness Fencibles	McPherson, John	Lieutenant	Lieutenant
Staff	Mackay, George	Brigade Major	Bt Major

N.B.—The temporary Pensions are distinguished by

War Office,
30th April, 1818.

Nature of the Cases.	PLACES WHERE, And year when Wounded.		Amount.	Date of Commencement.	
for wounds	Badajos St. Sebastian	1812 - 1813 -	* 100	1st September	1814.
for a wound	Badajos	1812 - -	* 100	7th April	1813.
loss of an arm	Navarre	1813 - -	250	13th December	1814.
for wounds	Salamanca	1812 - -	100	23d July	1813.
for a wound	Albuera	1811 - -	300	16th May	1812.
for a wound	Pampeluna	1813 - -	* 300	27th July	1814.
for a wound	Toulouse	1814 - -	* 250	11th April	1815.
for a wound	Carrion	1812 - -	100	26th October	1813.
for a wound	Aire	1814 - -	* 100	3d March	1815.
for a wound	Asperne	1814 - -	* 100	4th January	1815.
loss of an eye and ear	Seville	1812 - -	350	28th August	1813.
for a wound	Guadelete	1812 - -	* 300	2d June	1813.
for a wound	Ireland	1801 - -	* 70	25th December	1811.
Injury sustained in the performance of military duty	Dublin	1815 - -	* 100	14th April	1816.

an Asterisk * before the Sums.

PALMERSTON.

RETURN OF THE NAMES OF THE OFFICERS
IN THE ARMY,

Who receive PENSIONS for the loss of Limbs, or for Wounds; specifying, the Rank they held at the time they were wounded, their present Rank, the nature of the Cases, the Places where, and the year when wounded, the amount of their Pensions, and the Dates from which they commence.

War-Office,
30th April 1818.

PALMERSTON.

Ordered, by The House of Commons, *to be Printed*,
14 *May* 1818.

www.ingramcontent.com/pod-product-compliance
Lightning Source LLC
Chambersburg PA
CBHW041700090426
42743CB00025B/3491